PRAISE FOR
Lives of American Women

"Finally! The majority of students—by which I mean women—will have the opportunity to read biographies of women from our nation's past. (Men can read them too, of course!) The 'Lives of American Women' series features an eclectic collection of books, readily accessible to students who will be able to see the contributions of women in many fields over the course of our history. Long overdue, these books will be a valuable resource for teachers, students, and the public at large."

—COKIE ROBERTS,
author of *Founding Mothers* and *Ladies of Liberty*

"Just what any professor wants: books that will intrigue, inform, and fascinate students! These short, readable biographies of American women—specifically designed for classroom use—give instructors an appealing new option to assign to their history students."

—MARY BETH NORTON,
Mary Donlon Alger Professor of American History,
Cornell University

"For educators keen to include women in the American story, but hampered by the lack of thoughtful, concise scholarship, here comes 'Lives of American Women,' embracing Abigail Adams's counsel to John— 'remember the ladies.' And high time, too!"

—LESLEY S. HERRMANN,
Executive Director, The Gilder Lehrman
Institute of American History

"Students both in the general survey course and in specialized offerings like my course on U.S. women's history can get a great understanding of an era from a short biography. Learning a lot about a single but complex character really helps to deepen appreciation of what women's lives were like in the past."

—PATRICIA CLINE COHEN,
University of California, Santa Barbara

"Biographies are, indeed, back. Not only will students read them, biographies provide an easy way to demonstrate particularly important historical themes or ideas. . . . Undergraduate readers will be challenged to think more deeply about what it means to be a woman, citizen, and political actor. . . . I am eager to use this in my undergraduate survey and specialty course."

—JENNIFER THIGPEN,
Washington State University, Pullman

"These books are, above all, fascinating stories that will engage and inspire readers. They offer a glimpse into the lives of key women in history who either defied tradition or who successfully maneuvered in a man's world to make an impact. The stories of these vital contributors to American history deliver just the right formula for instructors looking to provide a more complicated and nuanced view of history."

—ROSANNE LICHATIN,
2005 Gilder Lehrman Preserve
American History Teacher of the Year

"The *Lives of American Women* authors raise all of the big issues I want my classes to confront—and deftly fold their arguments into riveting narratives that maintain students' excitement."

—WOODY HOLTON,
author of *Abigail Adams*

Lives of American Women

Carol Berkin, Series Editor

Westview Press is pleased to launch Lives of American Women. Selected and edited by renowned women's historian Carol Berkin, these brief, affordably priced biographies are designed for use in undergraduate courses. Rather than a comprehensive approach, each biography focuses instead on a particular aspect of a woman's life that is emblematic of her time, or which made her a pivotal figure in the era. The emphasis is on a "good read," featuring accessible writing and compelling narratives, without sacrificing sound scholarship and academic integrity. Primary sources at the end of each biography reveal the subject's perspective in her own words. Study Questions and an Annotated Bibliography support the student reader.

Dolley Madison

The Problem of National Unity

CATHERINE ALLGOR

University of California, Riverside

LIVES OF AMERICAN WOMEN
Carol Berkin, Series Editor

**WESTVIEW
PRESS**

A Member of the Perseus Books Group

B
mad

Westview Press was founded in 1975 in Boulder, Colorado, by
notable publisher and intellectual Fred Praeger. Westview Press
continues to publish scholarly titles and high-quality undergraduate-
and graduate-level textbooks in core social science disciplines. With
books developed, written, and edited with the needs of serious
nonfiction readers, professors, and students in mind, Westview Press
honors its long history of publishing books that matter.

Copyright © 2013 by Westview Press

Published by Westview Press,
A Member of the Perseus Books Group

All rights reserved. Printed in the United States of America.
No part of this book may be reproduced in any manner whatsoever
without written permission except in the case of brief quotations
embodied in critical articles and reviews. For information, address
Westview Press, 2465 Central Avenue, Boulder, CO 80301.

Find us on the World Wide Web at www.westviewpress.com.
Every effort has been made to secure required permissions for all text,
images, maps, and other art reprinted in this volume.

Westview Press books are available at special discounts for bulk
purchases in the United States by corporations, institutions, and
other organizations. For more information, please contact the Special
Markets Department at the Perseus Books Group, 2300 Chestnut
Street, Suite 200, Philadelphia, PA 19103, or call (800) 810-4145,
ext. 5000, or e-mail special.markets@perseusbooks.com.

Designed by Brent Wilcox
A CIP catalog record for the print version of this book is available
from the Library of Congress
PB ISBN: 978-0-8133-4759-2
EBOOK ISBN: 978-0-8133-4760-8

10 9 8 7 6 5 4 3 2 1

CONTENTS

Contents

SERIES EDITOR'S FOREWORD

For contemporary Americans, it is often tempting to look back with nostalgia on the early years of our nation. We stand reverently before the portraits and statutes of national statesmen like Washington, Jefferson, Adams, and Hamilton and admire them for their optimism, their clear vision, and their confidence that this bold experiment in representative government would endure. These members of our founding generation would surely delight in our admiration, but would they recognize themselves or their colleagues in the myths we spin about them? Surely not. Most of the men who wrote the Constitution believed that the republic it established would last little more than a decade. They had reason to be anxious: in the 1790s and early 1800s they faced diplomatic crises with foreign countries, domestic uprisings, and ultimately a second war with their former mother country, Great Britain. But perhaps their greatest challenge was how to forge an *American* identity that would knit the separate, often competitive states together into a true nation.

One central figure in forging that national identity was neither a senator nor a congressman, not a political philosopher or an author of learned political treatises. In fact, the person who did the most to spark national pride and to establish a national political culture had no formal political power at all. Her name was Dolley Madison.

Dolley Payne Todd Madison was born in 1768 in the midst of a growing colonial protest against the mother country that would lead to a war for independence. In 1787, she was old enough to follow news of the excitement and suspicion that surrounded the meeting of what we today call the Constitutional Convention. By the time George Washington's first administration ended, Dolley had married, borne two children, and lost both her husband and a son in a deadly yellow fever epidemic. As Washington's second term began, she remarried, this time to a Virginia statesman seventeen years her senior, known to friends as Jemmy Madison and to the nation as the "father of the constitution." When James Madison became the nation's fourth president, Dolley was his companion, his advisor—and his greatest political asset.

If James Madison created the nation's frame of government, Dolley Madison established the political culture that made it work. In telling her story, Catherine Allgor provides us a window onto the difficult challenge of turning the "United States of America" into a singular entity rather than a collection of separate entities. Men and women of the early republic wrote, "The United States *are*"; Dolley Payne Todd Madison persuaded them to write, "The United States *is*." As outgoing and charming as her husband was shy and somber, Dolley Madison understood the need to establish a distinctive American style as a first step in establishing a unique American identity. From the furniture she chose for the White House to the fashions she wore to the food she put on her table, she proclaimed a pride in the young nation that buoyed the spirits of its citizens and set an example for them to follow. More importantly, she knew the value of informal settings in fostering cooperation between men of differing political viewpoints and competing interests. Senators and representatives might posture on the floor of Congress, and they might hold stubbornly to their position in committee meetings, but at an intimate dinner party or a lively parlor reception, they could be persuaded to compromise with their political opponents for the good of the nation. Dolley deployed her social skills as adeptly as the men of Washington deployed their political skills, and the social events, rituals, and ceremonies she created and fostered turned deadlock into compromise, conflict into cooperation, and provincialism into national pride.

Catherine Allgor's focus on the vital role Dolley and her circle of women played in fostering national unity and national identity reminds us that a broader lens is always necessary when we look at our past. Even in eras when women lacked political and legal rights or economic autonomy, when their realm was narrowly domestic, they were active agents in their own destinies and active participants in shaping the world around them. In examining and narrating the lives of women both famous and obscure, Westview's Lives of American Women series populates our national past more fully and more richly. Each story is not simply of an individual but of the era in which she lived, the events in which she participated, and the experiences she shared with her contemporaries. Some of these women will be familiar to the reader; others may not appear at all in the history books that focus on the powerful, the brilliant, or the privileged. But each of these women is worth knowing. In their personal odysseys, American history comes alive.

Carol Berkin

AUTHOR'S PREFACE

I have known the name Dolly Madison since I was a child. After all, I grew up outside of Philadelphia, Pennsylvania, home of Dolly Madison Ice Cream. Holiday time brought the Charlie Brown Christmas special, sponsored by Dolly Madison Cakes and Pies, makers of Raspberry Zingers and Gem Donuts. Like many Americans, I knew the name but not the woman behind the sweet treats.

Decades later, when I was working on my first book on Washington women of the early 1800s, I ran into Dolley Madison again, this time with her first name spelled correctly. I was astonished to discover that not long after her death in 1849, Dolley had become a major advertising icon, her image selling everything from dishes to face powder to food of all kinds. Pictures of a dark-haired beauty, "Dolly Madison," adorned a range of products, anything that had to do with the home, hospitality, and femininity. There was even a sexy Dolly selling a brand of cigars!

Moreover, during her life, Dolley was maybe the most famous living American—certainly the most famous woman—in the United States. It seemed that anyone who visited the new capital, Washington, DC, wrote home about her, and newspapers recorded her activities. This was a time when women were not in the public eye; indeed, newspapers did not even print women's names, let alone stories about them. I was immediately intrigued. Why was this woman so famous? Just for being a hostess and president's wife?

I assumed, of course, that her fame, whatever the source, lay in her being a woman. There must be some reason that advertisers used her name to invoke American womanhood for 150 years. I was right, and I was wrong. Yes, Dolley's work, as her life, was shaped by her gender.

But she was famous for exactly the same reasons a male politician would be famous—she had political power. She was important in her world, known and discussed by people far and wide, because she had influence over her husband, she got government jobs for men, she had the ear of congressmen and diplomats, and, under the veils of wife and hostess, Dolley played politics.

In the years I've charted her political accomplishments, I discovered yet another nuance of Dolley's fame. The regard in which she was held by her contemporaries and her culture was comprised partly of respect but mostly of love. As I say in this book, she was widely hailed as a queen but also, as one congressman put it, as a "Queen of Hearts." People loved her, and she loved them right back. When Speaker of the House Henry Clay teased her, "Everybody loves Mrs. Madison," she promptly replied, "Mrs. Madison loves everybody." Love was deeply connected to her most important political project—the mission of national unity. What is such unity but love for one's nation?

As we shall see, the importance of bringing the new nation together was not Dolley's idea; the founding generation certainly understood how critical national unity was. For his part, Dolley's husband, James Madison, possessed many theories about the role of unity and how to achieve it. But when it came to putting theory into practice, luckily Dolley was on the scene. She cultivated her natural gifts of charm and empathy in order to bring people together—no mean feat in the contentious early republic. Men of the day had no word for "bipartisanship"; they thought only one party should rule. Unfortunately, two groups of people believed this. But somehow Dolley knew that the salvation of the system lay in working together. No one knew that the United States was going to be a two-party democracy, but Dolley prepared the way for that eventuality.

Dolley also understood the power of ceremony and symbolism. James might fret about how to nurture the people's "attachment" to their nation, but Dolley's actions were louder than his words. She created a presidential home that soon acquired a nickname, "the White House," and helped to develop Washington City into a thriving capital. In the president's house, Dolley initiated new kinds of ceremonies for a modern country, ones that stressed accessibility to power and social equality. She also formed her own political persona, one who could impart messages of legitimacy and reassurance to an American audience worried about the fate of the national experiment.

The power of Dolley's symbolizing work would be proven when the British burned the capital in 1814. The White House and Washington had gained such a hold in the American mind that their destruction galvanized the populace around an unpopular war. And Dolley herself was such a larger-than-life figure that the story of her flight from the city and her rescue of the famous portrait of George Washington would become the emblematic tale of the War of 1812.

In my life with Dolley, from ice cream to political analysis, this connection between Dolley's political style and its uses for national unity is the most important aspect of her life that I have discovered. I am so happy to share it with you. Dolley's story and the story of our young nation follow in these pages. Making history from women's lives presents special challenges; that story is also here. While this volume is both biography and history, it is an exercise in history making as well. Keep an eye out for the use of evidence. Weigh for yourselves my interpretation of that evidence. Maybe you have a different interpretation. At the end of the book, I've included some primary documents for you to explore. It's a chance to make a little history yourselves.

Catherine Allgor
University of California, Riverside

The author would like to thank the following reviewers for their thoughtful reading and their helpful comments:

Ginette Aley, University of Southern Indiana
Patricia Cohen, University of California, Santa Barbara
Stephanie Cole, University of Texas, Arlington
Heather Kopelson, University of Alabama
Jennifer Thigpen, Washington State University

Introduction

In 1833, Dolley Madison wrote to her nineteen-year-old niece, Mary Estelle Elizabeth Cutts, "We have all, a great hand in the formation of our own destiny." Moreover, Dolley added, the qualities that ensured a successful life were something Mary knew in her bones, or as she put it, "'at your fingers ends.'"

Dolley Madison knew something about making your own destiny. Born into the Society of Friends, she did not follow the Quaker path of disengagement from "worldliness"; in fact, she couldn't have traveled further from her birthright. Dolley became the most famous American woman in the world, celebrated for her good heart, her style, and her hospitality. Quakers did not involve themselves in governments or armies; as the wife of President James Madison, Dolley's political work took her to the highest office in the land. During the contentious War of 1812, she would unite citizens and the military as the symbol of America.

From her own sweeping life journey, Dolley knew to her "'fingers ends'" how much her destiny was due to her own efforts. But it is also true that circumstance played its part in Dolley's rise. When she married James in 1794, the United States of America was a fragile republic, more experiment than nation. National unity had been a preoccupation of the founders before the last fires of war had died down. The American Revolution was a rebellion against a king and a monarchical style of government. The success of the former British colonists, however, put them in a paradoxical situation. In the absence of a powerful king, what would hold this republic together? It is all very well to invest sovereignty into "the people," but can they be trusted to work together? Laws can only go so far—what would truly unite the United States of America?

On some level, founders such as Thomas Jefferson and James Madison understood that if no outside force compelled union, only what they called "bonds of affection" would tie people to each other. Put simply, the new Americans would be a nation if they felt they were a nation. But this was all theoretical to the male founders: what was needed was someone who could put these ideals into action.

This is where destiny steps in again. In 1801, Dolley Madison came to the new capital city, Washington City, and began a sixteen-year career aimed at unifying the new capital, the federal government, and, by extension, the nation. She would use social events, ritual, ceremony, and architecture to draw people in, showing them that the republican experiment was one they were all in together. When the divisive War of 1812 came, culminating in the burning of Washington, all of Dolley's work for unity was tested. In the end, the capital city and the federal government were secured, and the American people felt more American than ever before.

It was the perfect combination of person and historical context. Dolley needed the unprecedented situation of building a government from the ground up in order to fulfill her astonishing political potential. In turn, the government and the nation needed someone special to lead them to a bipartisan, democratic future. In the pages that follow, we will trace Dolley's path through her destiny, observing how her actions, and what people said about them, demonstrated the Madisons' commitment to unity. We will discover, as well, the lasting model that Dolley left for us as the Americans who will lead the nation into the future.

A NOTE ON NAMES

Naming practices for female subjects in history and biography have been a thorny problem for feminist scholars. Merely adopting the "male" naming form of the last name is tricky in an era when women's names changed over their lifetimes. At different points in her story, Dolley, for instance, would be called "Payne," "Todd," and "Madison." It becomes more problematic to call a woman by her husband's last name when the husband is also part of the story. This book follows a naming practice devised over many years. If a man stands alone in the text, he is given his full name or last name, following traditional conventions; i.e., "Jefferson." When discussing men and women in political partnerships, both will be referred to by first names, so as not to give the male half of the partnership the respect of a surname, leaving the women with the informality of mere first names; i.e., the Madisons become "Dolley" and "James." This is not a perfect solution, but if it is excessively familiar, at least the men and women share any diminishment equally.

A Triumphal Finish

The Madisons Leave Washington

APRIL 6, 1817, WAS A bright spring day in Washington City, the nation's capital. Down on the Potomac River, newly ex-president James Madison and his wife and political partner, Dolley Payne Todd Madison, boarded a steamboat. Their retinue included the enslaved people who worked for them and who managed the luggage along with Dolley's pet macaw, Polly. The Madisons and their household were heading home to Montpelier, James Madison's countryseat in Orange, Virginia.

Fellow Republican and Virginian James Monroe was the president now, and according to the other steamboat passengers, James Madison felt the weight of his term in office lifted from him. Usually reserved in crowds, James talked with everyone, cracking jokes, reminding one passenger "of a school Boy on a long vacation." As the boat moved majestically past Mount Vernon into the sunny Virginia countryside, dappled in the bright greens of spring, James continued "playful" as a child. When they reached Aquia Creek, forty miles from Washington City, the Madisons disembarked, boarded a carriage, and rode into retirement, the sunny day casting a golden glow on the celebrated couple.

James and Dolley had every right to feel that they were leaving a job well done. They ended their two terms of service by concluding the War of 1812 with an impression of victory and securing the Virginian Republican dynasty with the election of 1816, ushering in an "era of good feelings." They could have departed for Montpelier in March, after the

Monroe inauguration, but so many wanted to fete the Madisons that the couple stayed an extra month in order to receive the honors. The people of the capital and the nation were in a celebratory mood, especially about the Madison legacy. James's old colleague and sometime enemy, John Adams, was not known for his generosity, especially toward his fellow founders, but even he pronounced that the Madison administration had "acquired more glory, and established more Union, than . . . Washington Adams and Jefferson, put together."

Both James and Dolley Madison were celebrated in print, with gifts, and at "balls public and private." At one notable ball, in nearby George-town, the accolades provided the decorations. Salutes to the couple took the form of "richly framed" artwork, including paintings, and poetry etched on white velvet that covered the walls. After the event, the ball's organizers packed up the pieces and sent them to Montpelier, where they remained on display. Dolley Madison famously enjoyed social events, but, by the end, even she seemed overwhelmed, as she reported to Hannah Nicholson Gallatin, wife of Albert Gallatin, the secretary of treasury and peace envoy. Congress might be adjourned, but "still our house is crouded with company—in truth ever since the peace my brain has been turn'd with noise & bustle. Such over flowing rooms I never saw before—I sigh for repose."

Dolley's perception of crowds was correct. In 1814, during the War of 1812, Washington City had been burned, and there had been much talk of moving the federal seat to a more established city. Many congressmen had never liked Washington; the crisis of war seemed to provide the perfect opportunity to quit the underdeveloped city. Only after much discussion, and some behind-the-scenes maneuvering on the part of Dolley and the local population, was the decision made to keep the capital on the Potomac.

During the Madisons' tenure, Washington had acquired new status and importance to Americans across the country. A lot of them came to the capital, seeking opportunities at the seat of power. In a letter to her cousin Edward Coles, who was also James's personal secretary, Dolley, using spelling and abbreviations typical of writing at the time, marveled at the "unusual numr. of young men from every direction—in short, we never had so busy a winter because the city was never so full of respectable strangers." With characteristic emphasis, Dolley wrote that her famous Wednesday night drawing rooms had "such throngs, *you never saw.*"

With Washington City surviving attacks both foreign and domestic, it makes sense that the capital had risen in the public mind. What is less clear is why the Madisons were so universally celebrated. The conclusion of the war had made people "crazy with joy," as Paul Jennings, James's enslaved manservant reported, but the 1817 acclaim was not postwar euphoria.[1] Peace had been declared two years earlier, long enough for the nation to have figured out that they gained nothing from the war.

From the perspective of historical hindsight, the Madison triumph is a mystery. Among historians and presidential experts, James Madison was a mediocre president at best. Without question, his contribution to the founding was immense, with his role in the formation of the Constitution enough to secure his place in history. But most historians agree that his presidency was a highlight neither of his career nor of the institution.

Experts point out that James was not a strong leader; with his administration following that of the charismatic Thomas Jefferson, he could not even keep his party, the Republicans, together. He then embroiled the young nation in a war that not only could have been avoided but gained the United States nothing and culminated with the 1814 burning of the capital city by British invaders and the near abandonment of Washington as the federal seat. Little wonder that in the presidential rankings so beloved by the media, James Madison is in the middle of the pack at best.

So the mystery remains: Why were the Madisons so loved and lauded when the president came close to losing the capital city and maybe the Union? And what role did Dolley play? First Ladies almost never figure in presidential assessments, but, again, the laurels heaped on Dolley by the American public indicate that a focus solely on James Madison's performance may not give the whole picture.

If the famously grumpy John Adams did not like to compliment his colleagues, he did enjoy being right. No doubt he would be pleased to provide the answer to this historical mystery. As his statement quoted above reveals, the victory of the Madison administration was that it brought a sense of unity and togetherness to the country and its fractious politicians. "Mr. Madison's War," as it was known, may not have gained Canada or British concessions, and it may have been studded by military and political disasters, including the invasion of the capital, but how it

was conducted and concluded brought the country together and strengthened the Union.

Albert Gallatin, secretary of the treasury and peace envoy, was in Europe, but his astute wife, Hannah, no doubt imparted to him a sense of
the war's aftermath. He wrote to a colleague: "The war has renewed and
reinstated the national feelings and character which the Revolution had
given, and which were daily lessening." He correctly understood that the
experience of war under the Madison administration gave Americans
"more general objects of attachment, with which their pride and political
opinions are concerned." This process made the citizens feel "more Americans; they feel and act more as a nation, and I hope the permanency of
the Union is thereby better secured."

What people felt across the country was magnified in the capital city.
Until the 1814 attack, Americans, including Washingtonians, were apa-
thetic about the war and even their capital city. But the British burning of
the White House and the public buildings galvanized the local and national populace. Savvy political observer and local gentry woman Rosalie
Stier Calvert, who was no fan of the Madisons, hazarded that "the burning of the public buildings of Washington is the best thing that has happened in a long time, as far as we are concerned, since this has finally
settled the question of whether the seat of government would stay here."

This was good news for the locals and for the nation, as Rosalie correctly predicted that "in the future they will no longer keep trying to
change it and as long as the union stands, the government will remain in
Washington, despite the jealousy of Philadelphia, New York, and Baltimore." With "everybody and everything" "hang[ing] upon the government," no wonder the town seemed to be "jumping alive," with "tavern
keepers and boardinghouse people laugh[ing] for joy."

"Union" had been a preeminent preoccupation since the beginning of
the American experiment. The centrality of union is reflected in the very
name chosen for the new nation: the United States of America. The
founders and former colonists knew it was important to be united right
from the start, and preserving that Union would be their highest goal and
greatest struggle until the Civil War decided the issue. All of the major political events of the early founding period can be understood as struggles
over union. Shays's Rebellion, the Whiskey Rebellion, the Constitutional

Convention, the Quasi-War with France, the presidential elections—the common thread running through all of these watershed moments was the worry and anxiety that the compact of the states would dissolve. Significantly, in the early republic, people commonly used the phrase "United States of America" as a plural—as in "the United States *are.*"

As the leading intellectual of the founding men, James understood this better than anyone. Though he would write directly about the threats to the Union most often in the 1820s, in the face of the Missouri Compromise, the concern about union pervaded and underlay many of the political issues he pondered. For instance, in his musings in the famous "Federalist 10," one of a series of essays that he wrote with Alexander Hamilton and John Jay to support the ratification of the new Constitution, he performs a breathtaking twist of logic.

The nature of men (by which James meant men of the polity), James states, is not unity but factionalism. Nevertheless, even factions have their own internal unity, as they are "united and actuated by some common impulse of passion." Moreover, the kind of government James envisioned should allow factions; as no one group could dominate the system, contention between factions would give the society stability. In other words, the nation could be seen as a unity of disunities, each with a unity of their own.

When James wrote of union or national unity, he did so in a negative way; that is, he was concerned with how to prevent disunion, how to stay alert to potential traps and snares along the path to nationhood. But of course, though he did not have the temperament for it, the real challenge was to foster union, rather than just prevent dissension.

At its most basic level, "union" meant for him that the states retain their compact as a republic. But as a political theorist, James also understood "unity" to be more primal than a theoretical contract between state entities. He believed that for the republic to work, there needed to be bonds that held "men" (again, by which he meant only men, while assuming that wives would follow husbands) together, and though he did not have a terminology for this phenomenon, these would be psychological bonds.

James Madison was a believer in the importance of what he called "veneration" in cementing bonds of affection and unity among citizens of the new United States. Early in his career, when he was arguing for the Constitution, he feared that critics (including his mentor, Thomas Jefferson) would undermine the people's faith in the document, depriving it of "that veneration, which time bestows on every thing." Even the "wisest and freest governments" needed veneration to ensure stability.

History played its own part in the veneration process. Valuing "antiquity," James worried about the new nation's lack of history. Indeed, one of the reasons he delayed his publication of the notes from the Constitutional Convention was to allow for a certain passage of time, in order to bestow the psychological effect of long-held tradition.[2]

History and veneration were tools of unity. Some might view tyrannical government as the greatest threat to the nation, but James feared the corruption and self-interest of individuals. So the task was to implement whatever strategies were needed to bind people to each other and to the state, as represented by government, both federal and local. With "we the people" united, the Union would hold.

Ideas and ideals can only go so far, particularly for James, who often erred in thinking that if something worked on paper, it should work in practice. This tendency frequently led James astray, down a path where he held onto an idea far longer than he should have. When it came to the abstractions of unity, no one understood the importance of this intangible more than James. But making the ideals real was a different problem.

Characteristically, James's strategy for implementing unity was passive. Historians fault James for being a "weak" leader; his contemporaries did not disagree. For them, however, his presidential weakness was a virtue. The men, women, and citizen groups from across the nation lauded him for his restraint in war, his refusal to sacrifice "civil or political liberties" for "power and national glory," as one committee of citizens phrased it. This was as James wanted it. James Madison and his colleagues deliberately constructed a government in opposition to a king, one with a weak chief executive who would never garner enough power to abuse the people.

The ruling theory of the American Revolution and the new government that followed was republicanism (not to be confused with the Republican Party). Republicanism abhorred and feared the kind of absolute power found in monarchies; instead, a virtuous citizenry should exercise power. In republican theory, war bred corruption by letting a leader, in this case a president, take on more power. The old axiom "power corrupts; absolute power corrupts absolutely" could describe the founders' assumption about leaders. If wartime crisis allowed a leader to take on extended power, corruption—and then the fall of the nation—was the only logical result.

Accordingly, James did not let the circumstances of war impede his commitment to a republican government. He took on no special powers, either to crush political enemies or to extend the power of the presidency. Others before him had done so, as when John Adams used the threat of war with France to create the despised Alien and Sedition Acts, which were aimed at silencing and even deporting his critics. Every other subsequent president involved in war would use the exigencies of the time to extend their presidential powers. But not James Madison.

For the Americans who toasted and saluted him in 1817, James Madison's legacy was precisely that he had not been powerful and active but had held the country together during a dangerous time. His "weakness" ensured that the nation would emerge from wartime with all constitutional protections intact.

When it came to enemies, James had them aplenty. The disruption in Congress that James faced before the declaration of war and the internal national dissension after the declaration were unprecedented in American history at the time. Only Abraham Lincoln would preside over a more divided nation. Circumstances got so extreme that in 1815 a group of New England Federalists traveled to Washington to propose that their home area secede from the Union.

Fortunately for the nation and the Madison administration, the men of the Hartford Convention arrived in the capital city just as news of the decisive victory of New Orleans all but assured the war's end. Because James did not punish his enemies, as John Adams did, there was no need for prolonged internal reconciliation, no treason trials that would extend wartime bitterness past the peace. James Madison gave the country back much as he had found it.

Americans of James's time also recognized that his political style was consistent with his personal character. Even as most of his contemporaries acknowledged his substantial intellect, what made him a good president lay in more "personal" qualities of temperament—modesty, restraint, and especially self-control. James's sterling character, "philosophic" mind, moderate temper, and purity of spirit ensured that even so violent an event as war would proceed temperately. He would not get carried away or lash out, even as he was assaulted on all sides, by his own citizenry and Congress as well as the British.

In the era of the early republic, much political action was taken by men who were defending or avenging their personal honor, but not James. Men dueled to defend their reputations against real or imagined slurs, some uttered in private. In this culture, personal reputation was political capital, and men fought to their deaths to defend it. In contrast, James endured attacks on his honor, his sanity, and his masculinity, as well as on his wife and family, with apparent unruffled serenity.

People close to him testified that his public persona was consistent with his personal life. Many who dealt face-to-face with James in stressful situations affirmed what Dolley's cousin Edward Coles would later remember as his experience with the president. To Edward, James Madison was "the most virtuous, calm, and amiable, of men, possessed of one of the purest hearts and best tempers with which man was ever blessed." It was these qualities, Edward believed, that earned James his place in the pantheon of American founders, right next to George Washington.

Paul Jennings, James's enslaved manservant, provided his own perspective. In the first memoir of the White House ever written, he asserted that "Mr. Madison, I think, was one of the best men that ever lived." Like Edward Coles and others, Paul "never saw him in a passion," but Paul's experience of James is even more striking than that of James's colleagues. James Madison might have had reasons for keeping his temper and presenting an image of cool discernment before Edward Coles and other white men, but he would have no reason to pose before his slave. That he was consistent in his temperate behavior, even to Paul Jennings, testifies to the authenticity of James's public image.

For Paul Jennings, the measure of a white man was how he treated slaves and how slaves regarded him. "They generally served him very faithfully," Paul reported, and he himself "never knew him to strike a slave, although he had over one hundred." Nor did "he allow an overseer to do it." According to Paul, when reports of slaves' bad behavior reached James's ears, "he would send for them and admonish them privately, and never mortify them by doing it before others."[3]

The old saying goes that a man is never a hero to his valet, with the idea that servants see all the flaws in a man otherwise celebrated in the world. Paul could not have been closer to James, shaving him every other day and attending to his personal needs. Moreover, Paul's published recollections did not appear when he was a slave (and might have been under duress to praise his master), but when James was dead and Paul was long freed.

Still, James's reticence and restraint cannot account for the strong emotions and attachments that "the people" exhibited during the last years of the Madison administration. The outpouring of national pride and unity—both national and local—was not a result of James's principled passivity. At best, his political convictions and restrained personality laid a fertile ground for the development of strong emotional and psychological attachments to grow.

To understand the positive work for unity in the early republic and the developments of these bonds, the historical gaze must widen to include not just the small, modest man in the simple black suit that befit a republican president, but also the lady in plumes and pink satin by his side—his wife and political partner, Dolley Payne Todd Madison.

It is surely significant that Dolley was celebrated both alongside her husband and on her own. In fact, the famous Georgetown ball, where the praise was the decor, was actually held in her honor. As Americans praised James's modesty and restraint, Dolley's paeans stressed her warm and generous personality, her efforts to reach out and include others, and their effects on politics. One of the verses on white velvet compared her to the sun in her power to illumine, cheer, and be "admired by all." James's political colleagues lauded Dolley for the way her manners "encourage[d] the diffident . . . tempted the morose," and how she "suffered no one to turn from you without an emotion of gratitude." The mayor of Washington, DC, admired Dolley's "grace and benevolence that have inspired universal respect and friendship."

Others acknowledged Dolley's contribution to the recent war effort. Commodore John Rodgers sent his respects, as well as a "Mat . . . composed of pieces taken from the flags of all the vessels . . . captured" during the war. Members of the diplomatic corps, for whom nurturing networks and connections was part of their job description, always had special appreciation for Dolley's ability to create bonds. Lucia Alice von Kantzow, the wife of the Swedish minister, declared that no future experience in another country would "open more our eyes, enlarge our ideas, experience more the delight of natural, easy kind deeds, and kind ways, than what charmed us, in your flourishing, prosperous and fortunate country."

Like other diplomats before her, Lucia used Dolley to personify the United States, so that in the same breath she admired both Dolley's "many virtues" and "the gigantic strides your Republic makes to rival the best parts of Europe." Lucia praised James as a high-minded steward of the ideals of government but recognized Dolley's more active style. In Lucia's view of the game of politics, with cards "so well delt" and "well played," Dolley made "friends among both parties" and became "loved by all your country men and country women." In her role as the president's wife, Dolley "honored his elevated post," garnering respect "for your judicious conduct, and affable kind manners."

In the early nineteenth century, women's names, let alone their activities, rarely appeared in the press. Such public show was not considered respectable. But Dolley was an exception. Upon her leaving Washington, the famed Philadelphia magazine the *Port Folio* commended her for creating a social circle that "was at once the model of the polished life and the dwelling of cheerfulness." The author also understood why the creation of such a circle was more than a nicety: "At a time when the restless spirit of party covered every path with thorns," the writer acknowledged, "this lady held the branch of conciliation and she well deserves a place among those who endeavor to promote peace and good will." The political parties that the *Port Folio* referenced were the Federalists and Republicans. The *Port Folio* writer noted that in 1801 President Thomas Jefferson appeared to have offered an olive branch to his old enemies by declaring, "We are all federalists, we are all republicans" in his inaugural address. "In her intercourse with society," however, declared the reporter, "Mrs. Madison reduced this liberal sentiment to practice." Like the Georgetown community, the *Port Folio* also saw Dolley in a solar vein: "Like a summer's sun she rose in our political horizon, gloriously, and she sunk, benignly."[4]

James may have laid the groundwork for national unity, but it was Dolley who sowed the seeds and cultivated them. The Madisons were a brilliant political partnership, and their personalities became tools of policy. In their private lives, they valued harmony and thoughtful consideration above all, sometimes to their detriment. In their public lives, James's restraint and modesty, coupled with Dolley's amazing ability to connect people and to diffuse conflict, allowed them to pursue their goals of national unity and present for us moderns a model for rule strikingly different from the more masculinized and conflict-based styles of the founding era.

How they achieved their success followed the larger patterns of their political partnership. Dolley was the one who personified, who took on the abstractions for which her husband was justly famed and made them practical and concrete. Studying actions, then, as well as words, will tell the tale. Americans of their time understood that James's character and personality held the key to his political style; in the attempt to analyze Dolley's quest for unity, understanding who she was and what she brought to the Madison administration will be just as crucial.

A Perfect Match

Dolley and James Madison

CONTEMPORARIES OF THE Madisons and later historians have made much of the contrast between Dolley Madison and her husband. Historians, and even those who knew him, called James "shy," "bookish," and "incapable of smiling." They write of him sitting silently at dinner or standing to the side at one of his wife's famous parties, while "Queen Dolley" worked the room, charming all, putting everyone at ease.

At first glance, from the outside, Dolley Madison does seem like his polar opposite. James Madison was only five foot three and slightly built; his size made it easy for him to disappear in crowds. One party-goer remarked that "being so low in stature, he was in imminent danger of being confounded with the plebeian crowds, and was pushed and jostled about like a common citizen—but not her ladyship." Dolley was tall, almost five foot eight, and with a commanding, womanly figure. Where she glowed with the rosiness that signaled good health (though it was whispered that some of that healthy color was applied from a box), James sported a "tawny" complexion, the result of, so people said, a life of sedentary study.

James favored the simple dress of the revolutionary era and must have seemed almost quaint with his powdered hair, breeches, stockings, and buckled shoes. Dolley, on the other hand, not only wore the latest fashions from Europe and the best American seamstresses but adapted them to create an almost royal, unquestionably lavish persona. She was not above wearing satin and ermine ensembles, topped with suspiciously crown-like headdresses. Her famous turbans were a good example of how she used fashion to stand out. Dolley did not invent the turban, but she wore them so often and to such good effect that they became her trademark. She often attached tall plumes to them; if James was lost in the plebian crowds, Dolley's waving plumes marked her location, beckoning all to join her.

But such differences were only skin deep. Both James and Dolley were more complicated, more human than the depictions left of them. More important was not how they were superficially different, but how profoundly alike. They were, at the core, peaceable people, who avoided confrontation whenever possible. Both valued harmony in their domestic and professional lives. Put poetically, the need for harmony and unity was a topic on which they were at one, and they shaped their politics accordingly.

Historians love to ponder whether people make circumstances or whether circumstances make people. The answer to that is probably both, but in this case, it was fortunate for the nation in the early years of its existence that these two people who shared values of harmony and unity came along. And of course, circumstances challenged Dolley and James to rise to meet them, to put their values into action. Understanding Dolley and James as unity builders depends on recovering as much as possible who these two people really were. As is often the case, the characters they brought to public service were deeply influenced by their backgrounds.

When James Madison was born on March 16, 1751, he came into a world that had a position for him, one at the top of his culture. His paternal family came to the New World as "Maddisons" in the seventeenth century, and though they eventually lost one *d*, they gained land and reputation. Though the family had only been in Virginia for several generations, it was enough to make the Madisons landed gentry. James's father, James Madison Sr., was the wealthiest landowner in Orange County, Virginia, ruling over an empire of land, tobacco, and slaves. Hs mother, Nelly Conway, also came from a large, well-established clan, so her son James grew up in a world of family, enjoying security and stability.

As the first son and eldest child, James was the first in the family and in a world of male privilege and hierarchy. Following the patriarchal ideal, James was destined to be his father's successor, and though his adult life took him far from the fields of Orange County, the wealth generated by the land and enslaved labor supported his efforts, whether as a student or as a president. Houses and homesteads played their own parts in this hierarchical culture, and when James was very small, James Madison Sr. built an estate, Montpelier, for his family, a half-mile away from his own father's house. Following the script laid out for him, James Jr. would bring his bride to this house and, on his father's death, would inherit it, in proper patriarchal fashion.

These Virginians' sense of privilege and power as well as absolute surety of their place in the world are almost unimaginable to modern minds. In our world, millionaires and celebrities rise and fall, moving through cycles in their wealth, power, and prestige. Except for super-models and star athletes, we don't consider the elite of our culture to be biologically or fundamentally superior to the rest of us. Part of the American dream is that even the humblest born can rise to high status— can even be the president. For elite white males in eighteenth-century Virginia, their place at the top of the food chain seemed unshakeable. They knew who they were because they had generations of power behind them; they and their "lessers" believed that they were "to the manner born," that is, leaders by blood. James's destiny as an elite and a leader was so secure that even when the unthinkable happened—a revolution of loyal British colonists against the crown, led by Virginians— his path did not change. If revolution prevented James from assuming his father's position of wealth and power in a colony of Great Britain, he would simply do so in a republic.

Still, James was not a perfect fit for the world of Southern slaveholding gentry. He was often ill, prone to unidentifiable nervous disorders; add to this his short stature, and James seemed sickly and weak. Since James lived to be eighty-five, it is not clear what these disorders were, but what is most relevant is that James feared an early death and made life decisions according to his fears. His lack of vigorous masculinity mattered in his world. The South, especially Virginia, was already developing a culture that put a premium on physical strength and a model of aggressive maleness that seemed extreme, even within a much larger Western context that valued the masculine over the feminine.

The model of Southern masculinity grew out of the needs of a system that used forced labor. In a slave society, violence, real or threatened, must underlie the entire culture, to be always ready to hand. Social order is valued in all societies but is even more crucial in slave societies; white male domination through force was aimed not only at enslaved African Americans but also at free blacks, white women of the upper class, and white men and women of the lower classes. In this context, James was a man who learned early that, even if it was his desire, he would not dominate through his physical presence.

James's physicality was one aspect that made him different; so did his obvious intellectual gifts. The two issues came together in a decision that marked him for his life's path. As a child and young man, James was schooled locally and with tutors. As a Virginian destined for leadership, James should have gone to the College of William and Mary, whose alumni would include Thomas Jefferson, John Marshall, James Monroe, and almost all of the elite men who came from Virginia. But when the time came for James to matriculate, the school was suffering under a bad intellectual and moral reputation. Moreover, the college was located in the tidewater part of the state, one that was generally seen as unhealthful.

For both health and academic reasons, James chose to attend the College of New Jersey (later Princeton University), where he became absorbed in the studies that would form the foundation of his thoughts about the nature of humans and of governance. Upon leaving college, having crammed four years of study into two and then staying an extra year, James languished a bit in the Montpelier countryside, reading law, until larger historical events came to form his future.

If the Revolution had never happened, James would have enjoyed a dull, though prosperous, life as a British colonist. As it was, the challenges that came his way allowed him to find his vocation—politics, and specifically playing a role in inventing a new political system. He served the Revolutionary cause in a variety of ways, though his frail health ensured he did not see military action. He was elected to the Virginia Convention of 1776, where he presaged his constitutional work by defending the free exercise of religion and separation of church and state. He met his friend and colleague Thomas Jefferson while serving in the newly formed Virginia House of Delegates, and by 1779 he was selected as a delegate to the Continental Congress in Philadelphia.

While there, he gained a reputation for his conscientiousness and brilliant arguments. While many of his fellow delegates jostled for positions as leaders, James became known for his collaborative work within committees. So in 1786, he was a logical choice to attend a convention to be held first in Annapolis, Maryland, and then in Philadelphia, to rewrite the Articles of Confederation. James went to the proceedings intending not an overhaul of the Articles, which had been barely adequate to serve a revolutionary cause, but a complete reenvisioning of what the nation could be. He seized the terms of the debate, proposing a government that was truly national and also privileged the rights of individuals over the rights of states. Tensions between how much power to allow states and what rights and responsibilities were federal had plagued the nation builders from the beginning. James Madison's Virginia plan provided what he thought was the most balanced equation. Though the Constitution was the product of many minds, his contemporaries were not wrong in considering him the "Father of the Constitution."

At this point in his career, James's political work was varied, as he charted the path from revolution to republic, and scholars and historians have drawn many conclusions about it and highlighted many themes. But unquestionably, whatever the particular circumstances, James showed a commitment to unity. Early in the 1770s, James was one who argued that America should remain united to Great Britain. When it became clear that was not to be, he spent the revolutionary years and after building the new nation. He did not use the occasion for self-aggrandizement but developed his collaborative skills, bringing men of various skills and backgrounds together over his ideas.

It is important to note, however, when James wrote of "union" and "unity," the union he had in mind was of white male householders and the wives they represented. Like other founders, James could not envision a biracial culture, with free African Americans and whites living side by side. James thought a great deal about the issue of slavery, which makes sense, as James's life was profoundly shaped by slavery from his birth. The labor of enslaved African Americans made his lifestyle possible, allowing him to leave Montpelier and serve in public life.

He and men like Thomas Jefferson saw slavery as a "necessary evil," that is, an evil that they could not see how they could live without. What would happen to their way of life if they freed their labor source? And what about the freed slaves? Where would they go? How would they make their way in the world? No doubt James agreed with his friend Jefferson, who wrote in *Notes on the State of Virginia* that abolition would mean race war between guilty whites and resentful black people.

The moral dilemma of slavery plagued James all of his life. During a speech at the Constitutional Convention in 1787, he deplored: "We have seen the mere distinction of color made in the most enlightened period of time, a ground of the most oppressive dominion ever exercised by man over man." He admitted that when it came to the drafting of the document, that he and others of the Convention "thought it wrong to admit in the Constitution the idea that there could be property in men." Still, James understood that slavery must be protected in order to bring the Southern states into the union. Here's where James's famed gift for compromise had a darker side. He wished to abolish the slave trade immediately, but he settled on an 1808 date to end the Atlantic slave trade.

Like many a white elite who lived uneasily within what they called their "peculiar institution," James tried to counter the system's harshness with personal kindness. As Paul Jennings noted, he did not tolerate whippings or harsh words at Montpelier. He vowed to "depend as little as possible on the labour of slaves," as he wrote in a letter to a friend. The fact that he could not see the impossibility of his intention demonstrates a kind of moral blind spot in a man of otherwise immense intelligence. He could not see, or he could not admit to himself, that being a good master did not address the larger problem of resting a society on the labor of slaves.

In contrast, even though he had a mother, sisters, and a beloved wife, James seemed not to give much thought to the role of women in the republic. He could not imagine white women as anything but dependent wives and mothers. In this, James was typical of his time: no male leader could conceive of women as independent political beings.

In 1794, then, James was not just a congressman from Virginia, serving in the nation's capital (at that time Philadelphia), he was a national figure, a man whom President George Washington used as an advisor, a thinker who had shaped the framework of a nation. But when he saw the woman who would be his wife on a Philadelphia street on a spring day, James was just one of many who stared.

If newly widowed Dolley Payne Todd did not stop traffic, she certainly slowed it down. At twenty-five years old, and tall, ample of bust, and slim of waist, she was a striking figure. With her pale skin, hair so dark it looked black, deep blue eyes, and "a mouth which was beautiful in shape and expression," no wonder Dolley had all the men in Philadelphia "in the Pouts." Men stationed themselves in the streets to catch glimpses of her; when failing that, they would pass her, as she walked with her best friend, Eliza Collins, and then turn around to gaze. Eliza was appalled, exclaiming in her Quaker way, "Really, Dolley, thou must hide thy face!" Dolley would laugh and put up both hands to shield her beauty.

It was to Eliza Collins that Dolley turned when Congressman Madison asked to call upon her. Dolley famously beseeched her friend: "Thou must come to me, Aaron Burr says that the great little Madison has asked him to bring him to see me this evening." James Madison was forty-three, a lifelong bachelor in a culture where even the widowed remarried quickly. History only knows of a few women who captivated James; when he met Dolley, he fell as only a romantic can. James was uncharacteristically aggressive in his pursuit of Dolley; she seems to have been more diffident, perhaps because she had only lost her husband some months before.

But James's persistence won out, and the couple married on September 15, 1794, at the Harewood estate in Virginia. In the hours before the late afternoon ceremony, Dolley wrote to Eliza Collins Lee (now married to another Virginia congressman, Richard Bland Lee) of her impending marriage. The most intriguing part of the letter is the signature. When she ended her missive, Dolley signed "Dolley Payne Todd." Returning to her desk after the wedding, she amended the signature: "Dolley Madison!" adding "Alass!"

This rather dramatic amendment could be attributed to a lack of love on Dolley's part, and it is true that though the couple would become inseparable and deeply loving, during their courtship, Dolley was probably not as swept away with romance as James was. But perhaps Dolley's "Alass!" was more a comment on the seriousness of the step she was taking.

Marriage in the eighteenth century was more than a matter of romance. Background, family, connections, and finances counted as well. As regards finances, although she had lost her first husband, John Todd, as well as a baby boy, in the yellow fever epidemic the year before, Dolley Todd was comfortably situated. The letter she wrote Eliza on her wedding day contained no discussion of love or attraction. Instead, and this was quite a reasonable thing to do, Dolley talked of her surviving son having gained "a generous & tender protector." She also reassured Eliza that she had made proper financial arrangements for her son, forestalling any gossip that her hasty marriage would deprive young Payne Todd of his late father's estate.[1]

Dolley also shared important aspects of her background with James that they (and the outside world) would assume would make them proper marriage partners. She spent her childhood in the countryside with family (at least those on her mother's side). She, too, was part of the Virginia gentry, owners of slaves. Dolley's life was shaped by slavery as much as James's was, but her experience of the institution may have been less intense and more intimate. Unlike James, who had grown up in a household of over a hundred slaves, the Paynes counted nine white family members and five enslaved African Americans. Such a circumstance could easily lead an outgoing person such as Dolley to bond with someone with whom she shared close quarters, and evidence exists that she did. Dolley's niece, Mary Cutts, recorded that Dolley was close to her enslaved nurse, "Mother Amey," who was "tall and stately in appearance, always dressing as a quakeress." Dolley kept a picture of her nurse throughout her life; the affection must have been mutual, as Amy left five hundred dollars to Dolley in her will.

But, of course, Dolley was her own person, with her own set of life experiences that shaped how she came to the marriage. Just as James's position in life was dictated by his gender, the most salient fact of Dolley's life was that she was born a girl. Of course, other social signifiers mattered in determining who she would be in her world. For instance, she was a Southerner, of a good class, and she was born white in a culture that not only enslaved and oppressed people of color but associated "blackness" with all things negative. Still, her femaleness might play the largest role in shaping her personality. Being female meant that she would live her life with no legal identity of her own. Women in the English colonies, and then the United States, lived under a legal mechanism called "coverture." At birth, a female infant was covered by her father's identity, and then, when a woman married, she was covered by her husband's identity. The husband and wife became one—and that one was the husband. Accordingly, women lost their names and took the last names of their husbands. Because they did not legally exist, of course married women could not vote; nor could they make contracts or be sued, so they could not own or work in businesses. Married women owned nothing, not even the clothes on their backs. They had no rights to their children, so that if a wife divorced or left a husband or vice versa, she would not see her children again.

Married women also had no rights to their bodies. That meant that not only would a husband have a claim to any wages generated by his wife's labor or to the fruits of her body (her children), but he also had an absolute right to sexual access. Within marriage, a woman's consent was implied, so under the law, all sex-related activity, including rape, was legitimate. Only in a few instances could a woman escape coverture. One of them was widowhood, but only very wealthy widows could afford to live without husbands. Living under coverture meant that Dolley's only option for her future was marriage; how well she lived would be a function of whom she married.

Aside from her gender, perhaps the fact that she was a Quaker is the most influential aspect of her background. Her mother, Mary Coles, came from a Virginia family of Quakers; her father, John Payne, converted upon his marriage. Unfortunately, since little material about Dolley's childhood exists, it is hard to speculate exactly how Dolley's background with the Quakers, also known as the Society of Friends, directly affected her.

Certainly both Quaker history and contemporary eighteenth-century Quakerism promoted ideas of female equality ahead of their time. Because the Friends believed in spiritual equality, women as well as men could be touched by the Spirit and follow what they perceived to be God's call, even to the extent of abandoning their womanly duties as wives and mothers. It is not a leap to imagine that the young girl heard stories of these itinerant women, traveling preachers, who insisted on the primacy of their spiritual personhood.

But Dolley's relationship with the Society was tense, literally from her birth, on May 20, 1768. Though she went to great lengths (including lying) to claim that she was a Virginian, born and bred, she had actually been born in North Carolina. And not merely "on a visit," as she and her family chroniclers claimed, but because her father, perhaps fired with the enthusiasm of the convert, had just moved his young family from Mary Coles Payne's home region to the wild frontier of North Carolina, the site of a new Quaker community. This move cost the family something financially and emotionally; it cost even more financially when they left after only a few years. It is not clear why the family pulled up stakes and returned home, but evidence exists that casts a shadow of disgrace over John Payne's business practices.

Dolley, then, grew up in the Virginia countryside from toddlerhood to adolescence, an experience positive enough that when she had the chance as an adult, she happily chose to reenter that milieu with her marriage to James. Though the young girl was doubtless surrounded by loving kin, Quakers were anomalous enough on the largely Anglican Virginia landscape that her sense of "outsiderness" may have developed early. Quakerism also brought a kind of questioning not shared by the Paynes' neighbors. Anglican Virginians may have been able to live the life of slaveholders, seemingly without questioning the issue of chattel slavery. Because the Society of Friends believed that all human beings were equal, in the mid-eighteenth century they eventually arrived at the conclusion that slaveholding was incompatible with Quaker life. John Payne's family, including Dolley, must have been privy to the discussions about slavery and its consequences, setting them even more apart.

In 1783, when Dolley was fifteen, John Payne made the radical decision to free his slaves. As he could not farm without them, he transplanted his family (now numbering eight children) to a city—and not even a Southern city, but chilly Philadelphia. Dolley's nurse, Amy, refused her freedom and accompanied the Paynes to their new home. On the one hand, the City of Brotherly Love was an exciting place to be, the most cosmopolitan city in the former colonies, featuring diverse populations, new ways of living, and a rich material culture. On the other hand, John Payne chose the city because it was the seat of American Quakerism; Mary

Cutts, Dolley's niece and biographer, explicitly characterized the move as motivated by "one aim, the support of his religious belief."

Disaster followed the Paynes. In the space of ten years, all three of Dolley's older brothers had died, as did a baby sister, named Philadelphia. John Payne failed in business and, as a result of shady dealings, was disowned by the Quaker Meeting. In order to make ends meet, Dolley's genteel mother was forced to open a boardinghouse. Shamed, John Payne fell into a deep depression and died, but not before betrothing his oldest daughter to a man probably not of her choosing, whom she married in 1790. In 1793, Dolley, along with thousands, experienced the trauma of a widespread disease epidemic of yellow fever. For her part, she lost her husband, John Todd, her in-laws, and one of her two sons.

It may be going too far to say that Dolley could blame Quakerism for her troubles, though its repudiation first of slavery and then her father's business practices had brought her family to the city and effectively broken her father. But by the time she met James Madison at twenty-five, widowed with her remaining child, two-year-old John Payne Todd (who was called "Payne"), Quakerism had hardly been a source of unmitigated comfort. Even as a young woman, Dolley could not seem to find her own way in this religion in which she perceived (at best) high-minded ideals and (at worst) crabbed censoriousness.

The Friends dictated that members dress simply, eschewing the "status marking" function of clothing and as a way of indicating their position *in* the world but not *of* it. Early on, Dolley evinced the love of fashion for which she would become famous. Disturbed by the "dashing tendency of her character," as well as her caps, "the cut of her gown and the shape of her shoes," her "strict Female Friends" lectured the young girl on her leanings toward "the gayeties of this world." In response, Dolley, who would become famous for her refusal to confront others, merely smiled and then, perhaps passive-aggressively, fell asleep.[2]

The strongest evidence for Dolley's attitude toward the Quakers during her youth is revealed in her later life choices. Though the husband her father chose for her, John Todd, was a proper Quaker man, Dolley Madison married Anglican James Madison in 1794, less than a year after Todd's death, and was promptly read out of Meeting, both for her haste and for her choice. All evidence suggests that she abandoned her religious heritage without a backward glance. Moreover, though at the time she could not have foreseen her elevation to wife of the president, surely it is significant that Dolley not only became the most famous woman in America for "worldly" reasons—her dress, her entertainments, her sociability—but did so in the center of the kind of military-based political power—the seat of the federal government—from which Quakers set themselves apart.

In 1805, Dolley Madison returned to Philadelphia to undergo treatment for a tumor on her leg under famed physician Dr. Philip Syng Physick. His treatments left her immobile and helpless to resist the Quakers who insisted on visiting her. Nancy Mifflin and Sally Lane "remonstrated with" her for having so much company: "they said that it was reported that half the City of Phila had made me visits." Dolley confessed to her sister Anna that "their lecture made me recollect the times when *our Society* [of Friends] used to controle me entirely & debar me from so many advantages & pleasures." This must have seemed an ironic twist of fate. Married to a non-Quaker, read out of Meeting for many years, living a life "so entirely from their clutches," Dolley had to endure yet another lecture. No wonder, she confessed to Anna, that she "really felt my ancient terror of them revive to a disiagreeable degree."[3]

Quakerism may have also caused deeper tensions in the family. Evidence suggests that Dolley's mother, Mary Coles, the "born" Quaker, was less devout than the converted John Payne. After John Payne's death, Mary Coles apparently sanctioned the obviously "worldly" and advantageous marriages of her other daughters, even as one by one, each woman was read out of Meeting. Dolley's niece, Mary Cutts, admitted that John Payne's Virginia neighbors thought he was "a fanatic" in his decision to free his slaves and move away. John's devotion to his religion may even have created a distance between him and his family. Before their deaths, his three oldest sons were read out of Meeting.

Even in the ultra-Quaker atmosphere of Philadelphia, John Payne made an impression. "He was an elder," reports Mary Cutts, and "spoke in meetings and was called a 'Quaker Preacher.'"[4] There is no evidence that John achieved an official "preacher" status, but since Quakers testify when moved by the Spirit, Mary's mistitle might suggest that John

Payne made his mark by testifying more regularly or more dramatically than others.

For all of their negative effects and connotations on her life, the tenets of Quakerism may have also had a positive influence on Dolley—again, discernable in her later life and one that speaks directly to tracing her character. The Society of Friends believed that every individual, no matter sex or station, had an "inner light," the palpable presence of God. Accordingly, Friends rejected any distinctions among humans, even titles of address, seeing everyone in brotherhood with each other. In an era of hierarchy, this was a very revolutionary idea. In her public life, it was Dolley's very capacity for sympathy, empathy, and kindness that most struck people; perhaps this was her own adaptation of the inner light.

James may have harbored the same feelings toward "the people" he wrote about in his essays and over which he governed. But Dolley made people *feel* her empathy. Surely her greater attunement to people is a function of many factors, including her gender and sheer personality, as well as any Quaker influence that remained with her. But her kindness and sympathy, especially to those who felt out of place, may have also been the result of her own experiences of unhappiness and disruption. Whereas James had been born into a world of unimaginable security, she had not. His surety about his rightness in the world gave James an inner confidence.

It also might have made him somewhat complacent in his life. Perhaps his complacency about his place in society led to a lack of effort in his personal life. Not for him the risk taking and insecurity of romantic venture; before Dolley, he had courted seriously only once before, a girl he might have reckoned to be an "easy catch"—she was barely in her teens and the daughter of a political supporter. While many characterize James as shy, what they might have been observing was a reserve, a deep confidence that does not require the possessor to reach out to others.

In contrast, Dolley, who would be celebrated for her willingness to reach out to others, experienced a more tenuous hold on status, security, and sense of self. As a Quaker in Virginia, she may have felt out of place; as a young girl in Philadelphia, she was most assuredly an outsider. As her mother went "into trade," Dolley may have learned the deference of the commercial class. Marriage to a man as stable and settled as James Madison would not change her feelings overnight. She did not automatically become mistress of Montpelier; James's mother, Nelly Conway Madison, was fully in charge and would remain so for decades. Children have a way of cementing a woman's place in a family, but none were forthcoming for the Madisons. It was not until some time in her marriage that she found a place where she belonged—and that would be Washington City. When the Madisons moved to the capital city in 1801, did Dolley know that she had found her home? Until the Madisons retired to Montpelier, her time in Washington would be the longest she had ever lived in one place.

Dolley Madison left no diary, nor do her letters contain discussions of her thoughts and feelings, her own assessment of her personal influences. She does not dissect the effects of Quakerism on her adult life, save for the mentions, made in extremis, about the "terrors." Nor has Dolley left any evidence of her thought process as she contemplated returning to the world of chattel slaveholding when she remarried. As the daughter of an early abolitionist and as a former Quaker, did she have qualms? Or was she so relieved to be "home" again that she merely accepted slavery as a way of life?

Dolley also did not discuss the great changes regarding women and politics that were surging around her as a young woman and adult. This is understandable; Dolley no doubt spent her young adulthood thinking, as a woman and a Quaker, that politics had nothing to do with her. But just as historians assume her Quaker background played an important part in shaping her character, it is logical to assume that Dolley's political work was influenced by the larger discussion on the role of women. What was happening in the general culture is important to know, because whatever she imagined about her place in politics as a young woman, a few years into her marriage to James, Dolley found herself poised to become a political force.

The American Revolution had a politically empowering effect on white women of the elite and middling classes. With the advent of hostilities, these women were called on to step out of their prescribed roles and act as shopkeepers, farmers, soldiers, and, ultimately, survivors. This pattern of "female freedom through necessity" occurs in many wars. But the American Revolution was a war fought for universal principles, liberty, and natural rights. Not surprisingly, then, these new American women might expect some rights of their own. But aside from a few loosening divorce laws, women got no legal change from the Revolution. The strictures of coverture, which gave husbands total control over wives, at least legally, remained unchallenged.

But if the law did not give women any new opportunities, other arenas of life did. Winning the American Revolution was not just a political or legal event. The founders and the population at large understood that for the experiment in "pure republicanism" to work, the whole society needed to transform. Manners, ways of buying and behaving, attitudes toward art and education—everything was up for reinvention, and no part of society was free from examination.

The urgency behind such a mission was the fear of disunion and anarchy. If there was no absolute power, no king to cohere the country, what would hold the enterprise together? In republican theory, it was the virtue of "the people." With so much riding on having a virtuous citizenry, the founding generations turned to women. In a movement historians call "republican motherhood," women were told that in the absence of legal equality, they could have social equality and the crucial task of shaping the next generation of Americans. Before marriage, women could "entice" their suitors to be upright republicans, putting the public good before their own interests. As the first teacher of their children, women played an important role in instilling republican ways in their sons. Without challenging their traditional roles as wives, housekeepers, and mothers, republican motherhood endowed them with political purposes, directly aimed at unifying the nation.

The republican motherhood movement had some good effects: it justified the political education and awareness that women had begun during the Revolution, even as it did not sanction actual involvement in political events. Another good side effect of this postrevolutionary discourse was a rise in educational opportunities for girls.

Male reformers stressed the need for these new potential republican mothers to be educated not as men were to be taught, and not to fulfill their own intellectual potential, but to become fit companions for men and teachers for their children. But in the end, this was a consolation prize for not having the full set of rights that men enjoyed. Moreover, this discourse did not bring women together as a political movement, nor did it allow an outlet for women to affect real political decisions.

Underlying this new idea about women's roles was a body of work, one that James had studied in college, called the Scottish Enlightenment. The product of such thinkers as David Hume, Lord Kames, and Adam Smith, the Scottish Enlightenment postulated that manners—not laws—provided the basis of civilization and kept a nation together. By "manners," Scottish Enlightenment thinkers meant more than knowing what fork to use or how to sip tea. They meant the fundamental ways that people behaved and treated each other, how they ordered and monitored themselves. Laws can come and go, went the theory, but manners were longer lasting and more powerful than the innovations of a mere legislature. To the new Americans, nervously embarking on creating whole bodies of laws they were not sure would be accepted by the citizenry, the stabilizing and unifying properties of manners were very appealing.

Accordingly, women responded to this call and developed a variety of ways of acting politically in this era. Some wealthy women began voting in New Jersey. Other women, knowledgeable and passionate about politics, were called "female politicians." In cities and towns, "leading women" created social circles and events as part of a project to create a national set of manners. Hostesses such as Anne Willing Bingham in Philadelphia and Annis Boudinot Stockton experimented with European models, hoping to craft a social (as opposed to political) network that would unify the nation with a web of families, affiliated by blood, marriage, and shared affinities. If laws united through the head, these ladies hoped to unite the country through the heart.

In a familiar dynamic in their marriage, James was the one who had the intellectual grasp of these concepts. They formed the heart of his Princeton education before the Revolution; after the Revolution, he, along with other founders, realized that the nation had to cohere on a deep emotional and psychological level. Enter Dolley Madison, who had the capacity to translate these theoretical abstracts into concrete realities. James and other male founders set the pattern, but Dolley, along with other elite women, took on the task of weaving the patterns into the everyday lives of Americans. And Dolley would do so in the highest circle of all—the national capital.

3

"More Agreeable Hours"
The Secretary of State Years

SPRING IS A TIME for new beginnings. James and Dolley had begun their lives together in the spring of 1794. On a warm spring day in May 1801, they opened a new chapter in their partnership. Thomas Jefferson, the Madisons' friend and colleague, had been elected president in 1800, and he asked James to be his secretary of state. Accordingly, Dolley and James, along with Dolley's son, Payne, and her younger sister, Anna, arrived by carriage to Washington City, not only the new capital city but literally a brand-new city.

During the period from 1780 to 1800, the seat of the federal government was in New York and then in Philadelphia. In 1790, as part of a compromise that James brokered, the national capital was sited on the Potomac River, occupying "Ten Miles Square" in Virginia and Maryland. While developers and investors scrambled to carve out a capital in the wilderness (as some saw the country setting), the nation's capital remained in Philadelphia. The new city was to be named to honor "The Father of his Country," George Washington. The Residence Act of 1790 stipulated that the government be in place by 1800, and, accordingly, John and Abigail Adams moved into the barely livable executive mansion for the last months of their term. The Jefferson administration would be the first to rule from Washington City.

For the first few weeks after their arrival, the Madisons stayed with Jefferson in the newly built presidential mansion. Then for two months, they stayed in one of the "Six Buildings," which housed the Department of State, until the autumn, when their new house was ready. "Freshly plaistered," the house boasted four bedrooms on the third floor, a cellar and a wine room below, and a cupola crowning the roof. As the 1801 congressional season began, Dolley and James settled into what is now 1333 F Street NW, only a few blocks from the president's house on Pennsylvania Avenue, and began the most exciting and politically productive time of their lives.

If we look back with historical hindsight, the Madisons, Dolley in particular, seem to have been destined to rule over Washington City, but this outcome was far from certain. Though James had been a national figure when the pair met and married in 1794, it was not clear at all that he had a future in politics. In marrying him, Dolley did not necessarily sign on to be a politician's wife.

At that time, the fragile political unity that had coalesced around President George Washington was already crumbling. Washington's cabinet quarreled among themselves over ideological differences, and men that had been the closest of allies and friends became enemies. No matter that James Madison and Alexander Hamilton collaborated on *The Federalist* essays just a few years earlier, or that Thomas Jefferson and John Adams had done the same over the Declaration of Independence. By the 1790s, Republicans James Madison and Thomas Jefferson were the deadly enemies of the incumbent Federalists, such as Hamilton and Adams. Ironically, the Federalists were the proponents of the kind of "federalism" (which emphasized the power of the federal government over states' rights) championed by James Madison during the constitutional conversation. They tended to be from New England and the North, focused on commerce rather than land, and conservative. They saw the government of the United States as an improved version of the British system, and of their nation's allies and enemies across the sea, they identified with Great Britain. They believed in a strict social order, ruled by elites; their enemies cast them as "aristocrats" who wanted to restore the monarchy.

The leaders of the Republicans, Thomas Jefferson and James Madison, were also elites, but they appealed to the "common man." Though they assumed that the men at the top, such as themselves, would rule, they believed that small farmers should have more of a say in government. Republicans generally were from the South and West, with wealth based in land, and because they saw the United States as a new experiment in human freedom (rather than an extension of the British past), they were liberal. They allied themselves with the French, who were embarking on their own revolution. Their enemies painted the Republicans as bringers of chaos and anarchy, a characterization that intensified when the French Revolution collapsed into the Reign of Terror.

History has seen Thomas Jefferson and his Republicans as the more modern and, with its emphasis on the "common man," the more democratic of the two parties. Jefferson's efforts to create a class of white men who had whiteness and maleness in common and who could vote, however, had the effect of excluding white women. Though women had rarely voted in the United States, they had acted politically in many ways all through the Revolution and beyond. The Republicans, like Jefferson, believed women had no part in political life and belonged at home. The Federalists were no feminists, but for them, class trumped gender. Even though they seemed the less inclusive of the parties, the Federalists believed that women, at least elite women, could participate in political discussions and demonstrations and that their male leaders were accountable to their female constituency.

The problem with this emerging party system was that this was an era that believed only one party should rule; people did not recognize or understand the role of informed dissent, an opposition that helped to balance power. Unfortunately for the new Americans, it seemed that the true inheritors of the Revolution, and thus the destined rulers, were being threatened by a dangerous opposition. Of course, each party cast itself in the role of the rightful leader and the other side as a faction, a disloyal and treasonous mob that needed to be destroyed.

What no one, not even the brilliant James Madison, could see was that the new United States was becoming a two-party system. It would be later generations who understood that the presence of two parties, always in contention, provided the governmental system with its own forms of checks and balances. The value of a two-party system eluded the founding generation, and they never envisioned the United States becoming a democracy. The very word had a negative connotation in revolutionary days, meaning "rule by the mob." That the United States would emerge in the next century to be a powerful nation-state, under a powerful president and federal government, would have seemed antithetical to their republican dreams of central power checked by a virtuous citizenry. In the 1790s, what we now understand as the "growing pains" of a new nation, the founders saw as dangerous dissension, a threat to the new republic.

But in the 1790s, the Republican Party was less a reality than the beginnings of an idea. In 1794, Thomas Jefferson "retired" to Monticello, though he agreed to run for president in 1796. After an election that pitted the two ideological groups against each other, and John Adams and Thomas Jefferson in a down and dirty fight, John Adams became president. Following the rules of the time, the runner-up, Jefferson, became vice president, but the Virginian did not participate in the day-to-day runnings of government, virtually retiring—again—to Monticello. Following their leader, James and Dolley also "retired" to their own countryseat.

These retirements were clearly a pose. From their isolation in Virginia, the two men launched attacks against Adams that were, considering Jefferson's position in the administration, borderline treasonous. Together, the pair anonymously wrote the Kentucky and Virginia Resolutions, which, in the face of the Alien and Sedition Acts, asserted the rights of the states to oppose the actions of the federal government. Jefferson and his loyal lieutenant, James Madison, were doing more than poisoning the Adams well; they were also laying plans for the future. The first years of the Madison marriage were spent in the political shade at Montpelier, but as the cynical and often correct Adams noted, "It is marvelous how political Plants grow in the shade."

While James and Dolley were adjusting themselves to life on the plantation, and Dolley reentered the world of chattel slaveholding, the Adams administration raged on. Under John Adams, the divisions in the country widened as the president fended off both the English and the French. Jefferson and James took advantage of this division and launched a new bid for Jefferson for president in 1800, which they won decidedly. Jefferson regarded his election as a mandate, interpreting the Adams and even Washington administrations as a false start. In essence, he and the Republican Party would start the republican experiment over, and they would do so in the brand-new capital, Washington City.

So Dolley and James found themselves back in harness in 1801, beginning this new life in a new place. For the next sixteen years, they established a routine of spending their summers at Montpelier and the congressional season—roughly from October to April or May—in Washington. Dolley oversaw the innumerable details attendant on any move. She settled her husband and nine-year-old Payne Todd into their schedules of work and school. Following Thomas Jefferson's example, the Madisons brought furniture from their own home; Dolley decided what she needed to buy elsewhere. The Madisons also selected some of their own slaves to leave their plantation home to come to the capital. These included James's valet, Paul Jennings, Dolley's personal maid, Sukey, and coachman, Joe Bolen—country folk who had to adjust to life in a capital city. For the rest of the staff, Dolley hired slaves from other families and employed white servants.

As Dolley bustled about, trying to get her house and her family settled, she discovered that her job was made much harder in such a primitive setting. Though the plan for the city was grand and ambitious, the town was, as notably asserted by the city's designer, Peter L'Enfant, "a city of magnificent distances." L'Enfant, along with George Washington, had planned for a city that would someday feature magnificent buildings; in 1801, all one saw was those "magnificent distances." Albert Gallatin, congressman from New York, who arrived only a few months before the Madisons, reported that conditions in the capital were "far from pleasant." In contrast to the many amenities offered by former capitals, New York or Philadelphia, Washington offered "one tailor, one shoemaker, one printer, a washingwoman, a grocery shop, a pamphlets and stationery shop, a small dry-goods shop and an oyster house." At least one might assume that in such a rural setting, one would have fresh produce, but Albert complained, "We have hardly any vegetables," and that Washingtonians had to travel to Alexandria, Virginia, for supplies.[1]

It is true that Albert was only echoing what many would say about Washington for decades. They would call it "primitive" and "crude," dubbing it both a "swamp" and a "desert." Of particular note were the roads, which were few and bad. A good rainstorm turned them into mud, and trying to get from the Capitol to the president's house, "mud, bushes, thorns, briers" blocked the way. It seemed that everyone had a story of carriages and other wheeled conveyances getting stuck in the wet ground. But it is also true that more optimistic people saw Washington City as Jefferson saw it: a fresh start for the new republic. Many commented on the city's "beautiful situation" in the countryside, and for ambitious folk, Washington City, where everything needed to be invented or created, could be a place to make their mark.

One of those people was Dolley. Historians have long asserted that Dolley's role in the Jefferson administration was that of substitute First Lady for Jefferson. This was not so. Jefferson did ask Dolley and her sisters to preside at table when he had female dinner guests and his daughter and official hostess, Martha Jefferson Randolph, was not in town. Claiming this position for Dolley, however, obscures two points. First, Thomas Jefferson's style of entertaining focused on small, single-party, all-male dinners, obviating the need for a female presence, and second, Dolley was involved in her own social and political projects focused on bringing the various white populations of the city together.

After the divisive presidential elections of 1796 and 1800, there was a need for reconciliation in the nation and in the government, as Jefferson himself acknowledged in his inaugural speech. Hoping to bridge the ideological fissures caused by both sides' partisan attacks, Jefferson declared that "we are all federalists, we are all republicans." In addition, the new federal seat itself needed social and political structures to bring members of the government, as well as the locals, together. Lacking the long-established institutions of older towns, with none of the usual bonds that elites enjoyed in places where their families lived for generations, the new Washington residents and government officials needed to find common ground.

The government itself was far from a cohesive whole. Members of Congress, and representatives of their parties, were more politically rabid than anyone. The problem of the raw city only exacerbated the divisiveness. There were few places, clubs, or eating establishments where legislators might meet outside of the official spotlight. Everyone elected was from somewhere else and so did not have the networks and connections they enjoyed on their home turf.

The design of the city, following republican principles, literally separated the branches of government. Just as the Constitution avoided setting up a central consolidating power, Washington City lacked a city center, instead having multiple hubs with spokes emanating from each. The executive mansion, the houses of legislation, and the judiciary were deliberately set apart, isolated from each other and connected only by the treacherous roads. With "every turn of your wagon wheel . . . attended with danger," the total roundtrip for the stage that went through Georgetown, stopping at Capitol Hill and the president's house, a distance of about five miles, was three hours.

Those infamously bad roads led members of each branch to cluster in boardinghouses around their respective government buildings. To be sure, crowding members of government in small quarters had a bonding effect, but as members tended to cluster around shared regions and political ideas, the effect was the opposite of unifying. As Albert Gallatin reported to his wife, Hannah: "You may suppose that being all thrown together in a few boardinghouses, without hardly any other society than ourselves, we are not likely to be either very moderate politically or think of anything but politics." Boardinghouse life tended to inflame passions among those who disagreed or entrench those who did agree.

If anything, passions ran even higher when the members of government were on the job. Republican theory touted the idea of "republican virtue," which did not refer to sexuality or morals. Rather, the "pure republican" placed the public good before his own interest. The problem with this theory was that it presupposed one common public good; in reality, of course, people do not tend to simply agree on an issue—and certainly not with two parties operating. At the very least, there might be two versions of the public good, with each side seeing theirs as right and the other as treason. In addition, this abstract theory presupposed that humans acted like cogs in the machine of government and did not take into account that people act from many kinds of motivations and interests.

The theory of republicanism abhorred all things monarchical, including the way courtiers worked with each other to create political deals. To be seen "accommodating" someone smacked of the behind-the-scenes string pulling characteristic of royal courts. Collaboration suggested corruption, not cooperation. To seem virtuous, each legislator had to adopt the pose of "outsider." Not only were congressmen reluctant to collaborate, even with like-minded individuals, but they were also paranoid about even *seeming* to do so, and they were vigilant for any sign of cabal or plot on anyone else's part.

The House and Senate, then, were a collection of lone gunmen, eager to appear unconnected in any kind of way, calling out others as they saw fit. Savvy Albert Gallatin saw correctly that such posturing and positioning made getting the public business done an impossible task. All the finger pointing and quarreling, he declared, "embarrassed" the government in the eyes of the world and the American people. No wonder people had little faith in their government. In such an atmosphere of violent disunity, Albert Gallatin could not see a way "to produce the requisite union of views and action between the several branches of government."[2]

If Jefferson's inaugural speech was a call for unity, he had his work cut out for him. But the truth was that Jefferson really did not want to work with Federalists. He hoped to rehabilitate some to his cause; others who resisted he wished to be voted out from political office. As the purest of the "pure republicans" (as Jefferson thought of himself), he assumed his party would destroy the opposition and that shortly "Federalism" would cease to exist.

As a member of the gentry and a former diplomat, Jefferson understood the role of social events in building a power culture, but he did not want to share power with any one else. His primary form of socializing was his small dinner parties, to which he invited men of a single party. Dining and sipping with his fellow Republicans, Jefferson used these gatherings to rally his troops and to gather intelligence. When the Federalists ringed the table, Jefferson was able to keep an eye on his enemies.

The dinner parties had an air of intimacy; not only were they small, but Jefferson banished servants from the room, using his famous dumbwaiters and serving the food himself around the round table that kept everyone close. Some saw these dinners as evidence of Jefferson's hospitality, but it is true that by these practices, and by restricting the number of guests, Jefferson was in total control of the conversation.

Jefferson worried about the social scene for other reasons as well. He had distrusted the receptions (which he and other Republicans scornfully dubbed with a French designation—"levees") of the Federalist presidents as too aristocratic. That was his reason for refusing to open the executive mansion to large gatherings, except for New Year's Day and the Fourth of

July. Experienced at French and English courts, Jefferson knew these large events were perfect venues for people to serve their own political ends. He especially did not want to give political opportunities to what he called "unofficial characters," meaning courtier-like men and women. He had seen the power of women at social events in France, and he was horrified.

Jefferson's dislike of politicking women seems extreme. He imputed great power to women, probably as a result of his personal prejudices (Jefferson kept distant from all but the most complaisant females, including most probably an enslaved woman entirely under his control), but also his experience at the French court. That he blamed the excesses of the French Revolution solely on Queen Marie Antoinette probably says more about him than the queen. But it is true that Jefferson observed unprecedented female politicking during his time in France. Women of all classes were developing political voices, from workingwomen protesting in the streets to hostesses in salons influencing men in their parlors.

He heartily disapproved of women who "mix promiscuously in the gatherings of men." Worst of all were women allowed to "visit, alone, all persons in office" in order to obtain jobs for their "husband, family, or friends"; "their solicitations bid defiance to laws and regulations." Jefferson predicted that all the reforms proposed by the French in the wake of the Revolution would come to naught if they did not face the real problem: "the influence of women in the government."

Jefferson dealt with the fact that in his own country American women were carving out new political identities for themselves through denial. This was a typical Jeffersonian technique—to face unpleasant situations by pretending the reality one wanted. So even when in correspondence with a well-connected political woman in the United States, Jefferson could congratulate her and her female compatriots for keeping their "omnipotent influence" safe at home with a straight face.

One afternoon in the early days of Jefferson's administration, the ladies of Washington tried to defy his ban on them and the large entertainments they expected of their president. "Impatient for a drawing room," as Abigail Adams related, the ladies of the capital showed up en masse in their finest attire to the executive mansion—in effect, bringing the party with them. Jefferson would have none of it and, again, used denial as his form of resistance.

Dressed in spurs and his dusty riding clothes, he pretended that the ladies were merely calling on him and that it was an incredible coincidence that all showed up at the same time. In this guise, he could be gracious while making his point: "Never had he been seen so cordial and attentive." Though some accounts of this incident stress that the ladies enjoyed the joke on themselves, the truth was that he put them in a difficult position. "Calls" lasted only fifteen minutes, so though the ladies had planned to stay longer, they were compelled to leave shortly after their arrival. Though there seemed to be no fallout from Jefferson's display, this incident set the tone for the treatment of women at the president's house. Significantly, Dolley does not appear on either side in this story of social miscalculation.

By keeping men of both parties separated and excluding locals and families, Jefferson secured his personal power base, but he did not bring unity to the government or the town. Instead, Dolley made the home of the secretary of state on F Street a social and political center. Here she gave dinner parties, mixing political families of both stripes, American and European visitors, diplomats, and the local elite. She called and was called on; she hosted large receptions and smaller gatherings. Her entertaining contrasted with Jefferson's gloomy austerity, and many of the political tasks of cohesion and persuasion happened not under the president's eye but under hers. This was especially true, as James, though he could be charming in small companies of trusted friends, tended to fade into the social background. Before she ever became the nation's leading lady, Dolley was bringing people together.

She began by making friends with local ladies. Even while she was staying at the president's house, Dolley made an important contact with Margaret Bayard Smith, a writer and political observer whose husband had come to Washington at Jefferson's invitation to start a newspaper. (This was an era before the goal of objective news reporting; by inviting Samuel, Jefferson assumed that his newspaper would be favorable to the administration, and so it was.) Samuel Harrison Smith ran the *Daily Intelligencer*, one of the great historical sources for the workings of the federal government, as it served as a precursor to the *Congressional Record*. Through her letters and writings, Margaret Bayard Smith is the source for much of what is known about early Washington City and the people who lived and ruled there. All during the Madisons' time in Washington, Margaret would be on the scene, recording their political life. Margaret published her work in newspapers and used her observations in her fiction.

Margaret immediately noted Dolley's pleasing qualities. To be sure, she admired the "simplicity and mildness of James's manners, and a "benevolen[t]" smile that "inspir[ed] good will and esteem." However, Dolley possessed the "most affable and agreeable manners," which, along with "good humour and sprightliness," elicited intimacy and trust. Her power was irresistible; to know Dolley was to love her, as Margaret marveled on the connection she felt to Dolley and her sister Anna even at first meeting, "Indeed, it is impossible for an acquaintance with them to be different."[3]

Dolley did not wait for the ladies, local or governmental, to call on her. In a dark-green "chariot," with a silver monogram on each door, venetian blinds for the windows, and cut glass and candles (bought secondhand by James in Philadelphia for $594), Dolley braved the treacherous roads to call on everyone. "Everyone" included the local gentry families, many of whom had invested in the development of the capital city; the "official families," of which in the early days there were few, as men tended to leave their families at home and live in boardinghouses; and the sparse but visible foreign officials and visitors. Visiting everyone who even stopped in town, Dolley set a precedent for herself and all subsequent First Ladies. By calling on them, she officially "opened" social relations, allowing her to invite everyone to F Street.

And it seemed that everyone came. Part of the reason the house on F Street quickly emerged as the place to be lay in the lack of competition; with the president's house rarely open, it was almost the only game in town. But there were plenty of other reasons to crowd the Madisons' rooms. Dolley worked hard, pulling in visitors by a variety of attractions. In this mission, her sisters aided her. Dolley's sister Anna was a young woman in her twenties, pretty and accomplished, who drew the younger set to the Madisons'. Lucy, the middle sister, who was married to George Steptoe Washington, nephew of the general, often stayed in Washington. Lucy was a firecracker and a crackling wit, and the three Payne sisters, lively and outgoing, soon became known to Washingtonians as "the Merry Wives of Windsor."

If one were a lonely, wifeless congressman, such as Massachusetts representative Reverend Manasseh Cutler, an invitation to a Madison dinner party was an invitation to a world of talk and good food. Of course, there was a chance to interact socially with one's colleagues; perhaps for Federalist Cutler, meeting a member of the "enemy camp" over wine. Seated around the Madisons' crowded table, one might meet fascinating people drawn to the city by the presence of the government, such as William Thornton and his wife, Anna Maria Brodeau Thornton.

The Thorntons lived next door to the Madisons; Dr. Thornton had won the contest to design the Capitol building, and the couple moved to Washington to oversee its implementation. In addition, William was somewhat of a Renaissance man, writing novels, breeding sheep, and inventing a language for the deaf, while eventually serving as a federal commissioner for the city and superintendent of patents. Anna Maria was a well educated and articulate woman who rendered drawings, sketches, and blueprints for her husband's many schemes.

Further down the table might be Dolley's local friends, such as the Van Nesses. Marcia Burnes Van Ness's father made a fortune in land speculation when his acres were deemed necessary for the federal seat. Inheriting that fortune—about $14 million in today's money—made her the richest catch for miles around. When she married into the notable New York family of John Peter Van Ness, it was the perfect marriage of local gentry and official Washington. The pair invested heavily in the burgeoning town, starting institutions and developing real estate. As befit her sex, Marcia also engaged with Dolley in charitable and benevolent work.

In addition to these regular guests, a congressman might also hobnob with editor Samuel Harrison Smith and his influential wife, Margaret, a visiting inventor or preacher, and perhaps a diplomat or two. Dinner at the house on F Street no doubt made a nice change from boardinghouse fare. Manasseh did not even recognize a dish he called "Bouilli," a round of beef boiled and served with a rich, spicy gravy. He did know, and enjoy, the ham and mashed cabbage that followed, but could not figure out one of the desserts. "Two dishes which appeared like Apple pie, in the form of the half of a Musk-melon, the flat side down, tops creased deep, and the color a dark brown" may have baffled Manasseh, but it did not stop him from pronouncing them, and the rest of the menu, an "excellent dinner."

The good reverend does not record this, but things could get racy and sophisticated at the Madison table. Under the influence of wine and conviviality, James Madison told dirty jokes. Samuel Harrison Smith attended one party without Margaret, who was out of town visiting family. He related that he "rarely spent more agreeable hours" than he did at that dinner. Champagne flowed, creating a lively atmosphere, and James remarked that "it was the most delightful wine when drank in moderation, but more than a few glasses always produced a headache the next day." Ever the Enlightenment man, James proposed an experiment to discover how much champagne it took to make one hungover, "the next day being Sunday would allow time for a recovery from its effects." Accordingly, "bottle after bottle" was brought in. The only result of the experiment that Samuel related was "animated good humor and uninterrupted conversation."

Conversation was not the only form of entertainment, and champagne not the only stimulant. Dolley also passed around the snuffbox. Some ladies and gentlemen deplored the practice of "dipping" snuff, but it was a habit among eighteenth-century gentry. It was an addiction, as Dolley confessed to her sister Anna: "I'm glad you take no more snuf—but I must." The Washington company also gambled, with men tending to play a popular British gambling game called brag, and the ladies playing loo, a card game that resembled both poker and bridge. The sight of ladies gambling had its own allure; as one gentleman explained, when the ladies lost, they pronounced themselves "looed," saying "the word in a very mincing manner." Samuel was lucky his first time at loo, winning two dollars from Dolley and another lady. To Margaret, he confessed, "I felt some mortification at putting [their] money . . . into my pocket."

Of course, presiding at the table was Dolley. Reports on James Madison vary; it seems if the company were his friends, he could be jolly and humorous, even risqué. Most Madison guests agree, however, that he was often silent to the point of moroseness. It was Dolley who kept the conversation lively, and it was, as one guest characterized her style, "the frank and cordial manners of its mistress" that kept guests coming to her house. Manasseh Cutler admired more than the menu, commending Dolley as "very amiable, and exceedingly pleasant and sensible in conversation."

Even a simple tea party could be a glamorous affair. In Dolley's time, tea was an after-dinner event, and at the Madisons one could enjoy coffee and tea, ice creams, cordials, punch, jelly, cake, and fruit. Little baskets with raisins, almonds, and candied sugars wrapped in papers with verses passed among the guests, who also mentioned the treat of hot chocolate, still a rarity in early America.

Many guests followed the description of such lavishness by noting that the chief attraction was not these tidbits, but the mistress: "It was only in hospitality and charity that her profusion was unchecked." Even in her person Dolley expressed the balance she struck between lavishness and simplicity. Though often attired in "expensive and fashionable" gowns in the evening, during the day she also wore her simple Quaker cap and mitigated the décolletage revealed by her gowns with a modest Quaker kerchief tucked around her neckline.

The political uses of the tea and dinner parties were both obvious and subtle. Because of the size and configuration of Jefferson's dinner parties, a congressman might expect an invitation once or twice a term. In contrast, the Madisons might have an entertainment once or twice a week, one that included many more people and kinds of people. Congressman from Massachusetts John Quincy Adams might have found the conversation "desultory" at Jefferson's table of ten or twelve male congressmen (though he dryly remarked that Jefferson's "itch for telling [tall tales] was unabated"). At the Madisons, John Quincy attended with "a company of about seventy persons of both sexes." There he got to have a chance for a quiet chat, one on one, with James, enjoying "considerable conversation . . . on the subjects now most important to the public."[4]

What is significant is that John Quincy, like the admiring Manasseh Cutler, was a Federalist. Away from the political hothouse of the boardinghouses and Jefferson's watchful eye, men of opposing parties learned to talk to and with each other. Perhaps the most important lesson that they learned was that in a political culture that insisted that there was only one common good and one way to achieve it, political opponents were not treasonous traitors but well-meaning men who might have a different idea of the common good.

It is a tribute to Dolley that she constructed this social and political center under the Jefferson radar. It would be a misstatement to say that she did so in opposition to her leader. If Jefferson was famed for his hatred of confrontation, he more than met his match with Dolley, who had been trained by her culture to be a "lady," taking the path of least conflict. She did not challenge the president's social plan; she just gently, subtly made the Madison home the center of the town. Dolley may not have had official political power, but she had influence. In spite of the message of his inaugural address, Jefferson did not offer the reconciliation so sorely needed by his town, his government, and his nation. Reconciliation, at least on the capital level, happened at the Madisons', during "the sweet simplicity of Mrs. Madison's conversation."[5]

To truly appreciate the unifying function of the Madisons' F Street social efforts, one can imagine the scene like the opening shot of a movie. It is night. In a wide shot from above, one can see the whole district, beyond the parts of the city devoted to government. Though the occasional residence, such as the Tayloes' gorgeous Octagon House, is in the district proper, the ten-mile square mandated by Congress, more are outside the city, in the quiet, dark countryside. These local gentry are the powerful people of the town, but their fortunes depend on the "outsiders"—the official men of the government who came from somewhere else.

Moving in for a bird's-eye view, focusing on the government buildings, the camera would show clearly the republican layout of the city, with each branch of government virtuously aloof from each other. Around each government building huddles the little collection of boardinghouses that hold the official personnel of that particular branch.

At the center of it all—the district, the city, and the government buildings—lies the executive mansion. Unless it is one of the two public days when Jefferson throws open the doors, the house will most likely be quiet and dark, isolated on its hill. In contrast, moving in for a close-up of nearby F Street, the Madisons' is all light and liveliness, the heart of the city. Like a human heart, the Madisons' house circulates the life's blood of the town—politics and power.

4

The Merry Affair
Diplomatic Disunity

IN ADDITION TO THE local gentry and the official families, there was another population under Dolley's watchful eye: the diplomatic corps. Small in number, they were large in presence and in national importance. In the early days of the United States, only a few nations sent along diplomatic officials. During James's tenure as secretary of state, these included the United States' two biggest potential allies and/or enemies, Great Britain and France. In addition, Denmark, Russia, and Tunisia sent diplomats of varying ranks. Even as they concerned themselves with uniting a country and a capital city, Dolley and James had to contend with representatives from outside nations.

Obviously, the care and cultivation of the various ministers, chargés d'affaires, and other diplomatic personnel was the job of the secretary of state. But it was also true that the foreign representatives enjoyed a disproportionate influence in the larger government. First, in the early republic, the only real "business" of the federal government was foreign relations. "Domestic policy," as modern Americans understood it, hardly existed. Working with foreign representatives, then, could not be merely compartmentalized into a single department.

Second, in this age of little regulation, representatives of foreign governments did not hesitate to meddle in whatever domestic affairs they thought profitable for their countries. They freely lobbied for tariff legislation, courted various members of Congress, and, when it served their own national purpose, fanned the always-smoldering flames of division between the Federalists and the Republicans. The personalities of the players on both sides mattered a great deal. In an age of slow communications, these individuals did not merely represent their countries but embodied them. What became foreign policy was the result of interactions between individuals.

Coming from courts around the world, the diplomats and their retinues would have made a splash in any American city. As it was, in poky little Washington City, their lavish lifestyles and sometimes continental ways made them standouts. Reports ran rampant of the French ambassador dancing quadrilles with naked women. The Tunisian ambassador, the exotic Sidi Suleiman Melli Melli, charmed Washington women with his gorgeous wardrobe (including a papier-mâché turban), even as he scandalized the populace by presenting the president with a gift of horses, as though Jefferson was some royal potentate. He also requested that James supply him with sexual access to women, which Jefferson and James did, hiring prostitutes with a little off-the-record budgeting. James joked with James Monroe that the item was accounted for under the category "appropriations to foreign intercourse," playing on the term that meant, among other things, relations between nations.

Being James's wife, and one of the leading women of the town, Dolley was also involved with the foreigners. One might expect that Dolley, who only spoke English and who had traveled little, and certainly not abroad, would have found herself in difficulties. But she was an overwhelming success with this constituency. Much of diplomatic business takes place in homes and at social events, where people can establish intimate, trusting relationships. The professionals understood what Dolley was trying to do at the house on F Street, and they appreciated it. The various diplomatic personnel who dined and drank under the Madisons' roof did not just value Dolley's efforts in some abstract way; they personally benefited from the social structure she set up. No matter their country of origin, foreigners would have otherwise had a hard time establishing relationships in a town as socially undeveloped as the federal seat.

Augustus John Foster, secretary of the diplomatic delegation during the Jefferson administration (he would be promoted later to minister), noted approvingly that Dolley was "so perfectly good tempered and good humoured that she rendered her husband's house . . . agreeable to all parties." Peder Blicherolsen of Denmark was sure that Dolley smoothed his way in Washington, convinced that he would have been "poisoned" in his efforts "without Mrs. Madisons Generosity." In a letter, he compared Dolley to "Nectar, Divinities, Goddesses, etc."

As always, Dolley formed special bonds with the women of diplomatic families. In her early days at the capital, she enjoyed a deep connection with Marie-Angélique Lequesne Ronsin Turreau, the wife of the French minister. This diplomatic wife was a remarkable person, a commoner whose noble husband (it was reputed) married her out of gratitude after she helped him escape from imprisonment during the French Revolution. Dolley "love[d] the woman for her singularitys which are [s]carcely known to others." Dolley described her as "good natured & inteligent generous plain [meaning "frank"] & curious." They genuinely enjoyed each other, lounging in each other's company, "sans ceremoni," talking and laughing until Dolley almost "crack[ed] her sides."

Madame Turreau played a part in "finishing" Dolley, preparing her for a life as a prominent political wife. Though Marie-Angélique spoke "no english we understand each other well," reported Dolley to her sister. In matters of dress, Dolley said: "She decorates herself according to the french Ideas and wishes me do so two—." Generously, "she shews me every thing she has, & would fain give me of every thing." The two women attempted to overcome the language barrier by Marie-Angélique teaching Dolley French, the acquisition of every polished lady. As Dolley boasted to sister Anna: "You would be surprized to hear my improvement in the language." Marie-Angélique was an encouraging teacher to Dolley, as she "allways understands me," said Dolley of her struggles. Marie-Angélique did a good job, as Dolley became more proficient in the official language of diplomacy and so was able to communicate with all future foreign emissaries.

But Dolley also understood their relationship not to be merely one of personal affections but to have national and international implications. Dolley did not like Marie-Angélique's husband, the French minister, Louis-Marie Turreau. She found his treatment of his wife shocking, as did all of Washington. Western countries, including the United States, allowed for husbands to "correct" their wives with corporal punishment. But Turreau's cruelty to his wife went too far. Dolley confided to Anna: "He whiped his wife & abused her before all his servants." "I pity her sincearly," Dolley told her sister, who was in Philadelphia at the time, but begged her not to spread the tale: "dont breath it in your country as it will make them all [the French] so odious as he deserves to be."

Dolley also had a strong relationship with the wife of the Spanish minister, Carlos Fernando Martínez de Yrujo, because she was Dolley's old friend, Sally McKean, from Philadelphia. In their girlhoods, Sally and the Payne girls were chums, with Sally writing wickedly funny accounts to Dolley's sister about fashions and beaus. In their new lives as political wives, Sally and Dolley became even closer.

Diplomatic relations demand a different kind of unity. Obviously, nations are not trying to become one entity, but they have to make alliances and keep communication channels open, while always looking for ways to benefit themselves. When it came to US-Spanish relations, both Sally and Dolley played their part. In 1804, tensions around the Louisiana Purchase led to some unfortunate exchanges between the United States and Spain, in the person of Sally's husband. The governments of France and Spain had long passed the territory of the Louisiana Purchase back and forth. Though France had promised never to sell the area to a third party, and in fact, to do so would break a treaty, in need of funds for his imperial ventures, Napoleon sold the holdings to the United States. Spain and its representatives were furious with Napoleon and with Thomas Jefferson and the United States for their part in this illegal land grab. In protest, Martínez de Yrujo left Washington City, taking refuge in Philadelphia, without calling on James Madison first. This breach of diplomatic etiquette would have had more serious ramifications if Sally had not "covered" for her husband by calling on Dolley before leaving town.

While the Martínezes were in Philadelphia, Dolley directed her sister Anna, who was visiting her old hometown, to further mend fences by calling on them, instructing her to "Remember me to McKeans & to Sally say a great deal for I feel a tenderness for her & her husband independent of circumstances."[1] Dolley's claim to be "independent of circumstances" seemed to separate the official from the personal, even as it was intended to improve more than personal relations. It is important to recognize these efforts, even as they did not fully work. Despite the efforts of Dolley and Sally, relations between Spain and the United States continued to deteriorate; indeed, for the next two years, President Jefferson did all he could to force Martínez de Yrujo to leave without completely rupturing ties with Spain. The bonds forged by Dolley and the Martínezes went a long way to easing the resultant tensions, keeping the diplomatic conversation going.

"Foreign relations" also covered relations with Native American tribes, which were foreign governments with their own sovereignty. It was always a colorful occasion for Washingtonians, white and black, when the tribal leaders came to town to be entertained by the Madisons. After one such event, Dolley was preparing for bed when she looked up and saw "the face of a wild Indian!" reflected in the mirror. She did not panic, guessing that when the man left the drawing room after the party, he went upstairs rather than down. Dolley's social training, which taught her not to draw attention to gaffes on the part of her guests, kicked in. She pretended not to have seen him, went into the next room, and instructed a slave to escort her visitor out.

Dolley's almost instant success as a de facto diplomat is due to her own instincts to connect and attach; no one needed to convince her of the importance of unity through diplomacy. In 1803, however, Dolley played a supporting role in, and had a front row seat for, the clearest lesson on the consequences of diplomatic disunity in the early republic. Though she left little record of her thoughts behind, she learned a great deal as she saw the fiasco play out. The infamous "Merry Affair" had definite consequences not only for present and future US-British relations but for the unity of her country.

In 1803, all of Washington was agog. The United States was to get their first full minister, Anthony Merry, from the Court of St. James, Great Britain's seat of government, since 1800. Such an appointment marked a heightening of US relations with Great Britain and an opportunity for reconciliation and advancement. Two decades after the end of the Revolutionary War, the situation between the European superpower and its former colonies was still tense. For instance, Great Britain refused to make reparations for enslaved people who had run away to British troops during hostilities, while insisting that Americans honor pre–Revolutionary War debts. Great Britain also required that merchant ships of a neutral nation not trade with countries at war with Great Britain; acquiescing to this condition ensured that the new United States, via its shipping trade, would be well and truly entangled in the British ever-fierce and deepening war with France.

The United States' erstwhile ally, France, presented a slate of trouble for their own part, as well as complicating matters with Great Britain. The trade agreement demanded by Great Britain directly contradicted arrangements that the United States had made separately with France. The bloody chaos of the French Revolution, the 1797 refusal to receive US ministers, the X, Y, Z Affair, the Quasi-War, the rise of Napoleon Bonaparte—all of these French developments complicated the US position on the world stage.

Adding to the inherently complicated foreign situation was the domestic effect. The Federalists and Republicans differed on foreign relations as they did on everything. Generally, the Federalists were seen as British sympathizers, while Republicans such as Thomas Jefferson sided with revolutionary France. Though no doubt members of each party had sincere concerns, it was also true that each party used the actions of the European players to paint the other into various ideological corners.

The year 1803 saw Great Britain and France at war with each other and the resulting Louisiana Purchase, as Napoleon liquefied his New World assets to pay the war bills. Suddenly, the pressure was off the United States—or so it seemed. With the acquisition of France's territory, Americans did not need to worry about France's encroaching military and political influence in their part of the continent (a situation so troubling that Anglophobe president Jefferson actually considered an alliance with the British). Moreover, such a large infusion of land changed the young nation's status. More stable and more impressive than it had been right after the Revolution, the United States was in the most advantageous position yet to settle the lingering issues of maritime and trade rights and boundaries with Great Britain.

No doubt Great Britain thought it a propitious time as well, choosing to send a full minister, the highest category of diplomatic official, to the new capital city, Washington. Even the pro-French paper the *Aurora* declared that the arrival of the minister, Anthony Merry, was a great opportunity, as a time "more favorable to amiable and generous views" had never existed. But this was not to be. The Merry Affair could have been much worse—there could have been a declaration of war—but it was still disastrous.

Historians have often blamed Minister Merry and his wife, Elizabeth Leathes Merry, for the turn of events. The choice of the Merrys for the American posting, however, was not the problem. Anthony Merry was a diligent career diplomat who had dealt with Napoleon. His newlywed wife was precisely the kind of cultured, accomplished woman who would be an asset in a diplomatic career. It is true that if Anthony Merry possessed more of a sense of humor and personal flexibility, his path in Washington might have been smoother. It is hard to see what fault Elizabeth might have committed, as she behaved within the completely correct diplomatic usage that all nations (even the United States) understood.

The real cause of the Merry fiasco was Thomas Jefferson. Right from the start, he was willing to jeopardize any chances to build bridges or mend fences with the nation that could have been either the United States' good friend or its most powerful enemy. He determined to "reduce" Great Britain via the person sent to represent it. The reason the president embarked on this course was simple—Thomas Jefferson hated the British. Before the Revolution, he was a wealthy colonist who prided himself on his connection to the Mother Country. Along with other members of the Virginia gentry, Jefferson was also the first to feel betrayed, when his countrymen started to demand payment for outstanding debts from wealthy Virginians.

During the war in 1781, not only did marauding British troops pillage his Elk Hill plantation, destroying property and stealing slaves, but their presence caused Jefferson, the governor at the time, to flee. His retreat brought down charges of cowardice that would haunt him his whole life. When he appeared at the Court of St. James in his capacity as American minister to France, Jefferson was treated so shabbily by

King George, who turned his back on the American, that it permanently embittered him. He pronounced "diplomacy as the pest of the peace of the world, as the workshop in which nearly all the wars of Europe are manufactured."[2] With no respect for diplomacy and great antipathy to Great Britain, Jefferson was more than poised to make the Merrys a target and an example.

The Merrys had an inauspicious start to their American experience. On November 4, 1803, they arrived after a rough transatlantic journey in Norfolk, Virginia, where they spent two weeks recovering from illnesses and awaiting transportation. The couple embarked on what should have been a short river journey to Alexandria, Virginia, but it dragged on for six days. Arriving in Washington City at last, the Merrys expressed the kind of shock shared by other European travelers. Used to London and Paris, they found the capital unbelievably primitive.

Somehow, in this unrefined city on the Potomac, they had to set up a diplomatic household. They began by putting together two "mere shells of houses, with bare walls and without fixtures of any kind." The Merrys did not even have available water until they had a well dug, and they had to send out to Baltimore and Philadelphia not only for the delicacies they would require to entertain their guests but also for staples such as butter and vegetables.

As the two coped with the various inconveniences of settling in, Anthony Merry prepared for the all-important diplomatic presentation. Then as now, interactions between representatives of foreign nations are as constructed and choreographed as a ballet. This kind of rigidity is restrictive but also establishes boundaries and a "universal" set of rules and language, creating a common ground on which everyone knows how to behave. The first official event when a diplomat or minister arrives is the "presentation," during which the emissary presents his credentials to the king or president. The reigning ruler then formally "accepts" the minister.

Speeches on both sides, flowery but revealing, establish the "ground rules" for the nations' subsequent interactions and relationships. Dress and rules of movement—for instance, the applying diplomat does not turn his back on the monarch—were set and well known. At the very least, the presentation is a formal step, signaling the opening of relations between nations within an atmosphere of mutual (even if wary) respect. At its best, such an occasion can also start the beginning of a productive and mutually enriching relationship between two men and their respective countries. Up until Anthony Merry's arrival, Jefferson had followed the agreed-on protocol.

Accordingly, in December 1803, Anthony Merry showed up at the executive mansion with his credentials in hand. As per the custom, he was dressed in his finest clothes, both to establish the legitimacy of the government he represented and to honor his host. He wore a deep-blue coat with black velvet trim and gold braid, white breeches, silk stockings, buckled shoes, plumed hat, and a sword. James Madison, who received Anthony, later remarked that he was "bespeckled with the spangles of [the] gaudiest court dress."

James led Anthony to the room where the presentation was to take place. But Jefferson was not there, and when James went to look for him, Anthony Merry followed, thinking they were going to another room for the formalities. As the two were heading out, Jefferson entered the room from another door. This caused no end of awkwardness as Anthony, caught with his back to the president, had to quickly reorient himself, bumping his hat, feathers, and sword into the wall.

The biggest shock to Anthony Merry, however, was how the leader of this new nation was dressed. Later, anti-Jefferson Federalist reports may have exaggerated when they claimed he was in his robe and slippers and nightcap. But Anthony himself related that President Jefferson was in down-at-the-heels slippers and that his pants, coat, and shirt indicated "utter slovenliness and indifference to appearances." The pièce de résistance for Anthony came when Jefferson, while discoursing pleasantly enough, tossed a slipper in the air and caught it with his toe.

The scene is not without humor, but it is important to remember that this was not some instance of personal eccentricity or a Virginia custom on Thomas Jefferson's part. He had served in royal courts, but even if he had not, Jefferson, like many Southern gentry, was a skilled and gracious host. At the very least, his behavior made his guest uncomfortable, violating the first rule of hospitality. But, of course, this was not just any guest. Jefferson's "presentation" was his way of showing his and America's equality, putting Great Britain in its place. Anthony

Merry instantly got the message. He did not believe the casual act Jefferson put on, seeing his slovenliness as "actually studied."

Anthony was further discombobulated when, after the presentation, James informed him that he would be expected to make the "first call" on the members of the American government. Paying the first call was a way to convey honor, and, without exception, diplomatic families expected the locals to pay the first call on them. Even in American small towns, visitors could expect to be called on by locals. Anthony knew what his predecessors had enjoyed and protested this new, unprecedented set of rules, but to no avail. However, James then softened the blow by promising that Dolley, as leading cabinet wife, would pay the first call on Elizabeth Merry.

Things only got worse for the Merrys. Three days later, Jefferson held a dinner to honor the Merrys at the president's house. Thomas Jefferson broke rules of precedence by not escorting his female guest of honor, Elizabeth Merry, to dinner. Instead, he took Dolley's arm; taken aback, she whispered, "Take Mrs. Merry." Formal precedence established that the male host escort the highest-ranking wife, the next highest male following with the next-highest woman, and so forth. Other guests expressed their shock at what must have seemed the most obvious insult. Sally McKean Martínez de Yrujo exclaimed, "This will be the cause of war."[3]

The rules of precedence guaranteed order and that each lady would have a gentleman to escort her to her seat. Again, even in the smallest town in America, the male host would not dream of leaving the female guest of honor stranded. By taking in Dolley, Jefferson threw off the calculation, and everyone scrambled for a seat, forcing Anthony to enter alone, and go down the table, hunting for a chair. Perhaps worst of all, Jefferson had also included the French chargé d'affaires, Louis-André Pichon, at the dinner, a breach of the rules that forbade inviting the representatives of warring countries to the same social occasion.

The scene was repeated at a dinner at the Madisons' home a few days later. In this case, James bypassed Elizabeth Merry to escort the next-highest cabinet wife next to his own, Hannah Nicholson Gallatin. In fact, the whole party paired off, leaving the Merrys to escort themselves. One of the rules of society that governed the Western world decreed that husbands and wives not go into dinner together, nor should they sit together. That Anthony had to escort his own wife would have been considered outrageous in any social setting; that James deliberately snubbed Elizabeth, choosing to instead escort the next-ranked woman, Hannah, was outrageous gaucherie.

It is not clear what Dolley Madison thought of all this. Indeed, the women of the episode are largely silent, but when they spoke or acted, it is clear that they were uneasy with Jefferson's experiment. James might have been ready to follow Jefferson's lead, but it is not clear that his female counterparts supported him. Sally Martínez de Yrujo correctly categorized such behavior as a major breach, and when Elizabeth finally made it into the Madison dining room, she went up to the head of the table, her "proper" spot, and Hannah Gallatin ceded to her without demur.

Immediately after this dinner, Anthony wrote to his government, complaining about his treatment. The presence of French chargé d'affaires, who, Anthony found out, had been especially asked by Jefferson to attend, was cause enough for Great Britain to reconsider the situation vis-à-vis the United States. When Anthony had protested his treatment to James, the secretary of state, no doubt speaking for his president, replied that Merry was in a republic now and he had to adapt to American usage. Anthony suspected, quite correctly, however, that such innovations had been instituted just for him (no other diplomatic presence had suffered so) and that they were intended as an insult to the country he represented. He requested instructions from his government on how to proceed; in the worst case scenario, the Merrys could have been recalled, breaking off relations between the two nations.

In the meantime, Jefferson and James Madison may have realized that they went too far. As British secretary Augustus John Foster said, "Mr. Jefferson and Mr. Madison were too much of the gentleman not to feel ashamed of what they were doing and consequently did it awkwardly, as people must do who affect bad manners for a particular object." The two men scrambled to provide an after-the-fact justification, writing to the American minister to England, Rufus King, for information about procedures. King, as well as James, understood that, Jeffersonian notions of republican equality aside, there had to be rules of behavior and that informality signaled a lack of seriousness and legitimacy in the national experiment. Rather than apologize, Jefferson issued a declaration, "The Cannons of Etiquette" (he meant, of course, "canons"; perhaps his martial mistake was a slip of the subconscious), which dispensed with most of the rule of precedence, declaring equality to be the rule of personal and diplomatic relations.

The one exception was for foreigners, who were to subordinate themselves to local officials in paying the first call. The only concession to "ancient usage" would be the "gentlemen in mass giving precedence to the ladies in mass" when moving between rooms. In his investigations, James had come upon a very particular instance within old English court practice. The large, elaborate, and often arcane structure of etiquette occasionally allowed "company" complete freedom of movement, usually at a large event, "pell mell." James and Jefferson adopted this phrase to give their unprecedented etiquette some justification. For their version, Jefferson and James reverted to the practice's French origins, calling it "pele mele," meaning, "to tumble."[4]

This too-little, too-late justification did not sway the Merrys, who pointed out that they should have been given the new rules on their arrival. Jefferson had no reply to this, as, of course, the rules had not existed. In truth, "pele mele" never really took off, and the older practices gradually came back. But the Merry Affair, though it, too, died down, had some deleterious effects, ones disruptive of the very unity successful diplomacy was supposed to foster.

The first result came within the first weeks after the initial salvos in the etiquette war. Not wishing to subject his wife to more insult in an uncertain atmosphere, Anthony decided to do only the bare minimum of his duties and insisted on attending only large official functions and by himself. The couple refused to dine at the president's house until he apologized. Appearing only when absolutely necessary cut down the numbers of opportunities that the representative from Great Britain had to connect with members of the government. By excusing Elizabeth, this new policy was doubly deleterious, as women were an important part of the diplomatic process. Their presence at social events created the bonds of trust needed for diplomatic relations.

In fact, when Jefferson and James learned of Anthony's decision, they tried to persuade him to attend official dinners anyway, without his wife. In his more casual dinners with congressmen Jefferson could get away with not inviting women; excluding wives from diplomatic dinners was such an astounding proposition, from a diplomatic point of view, that Anthony replied that he would have to seek counsel on the matter. Jefferson reacted snappishly: "I shall be highly honored when the king of England is good enough to let Mr. Merry come and eat my soup."

Jefferson had a lot to say about Anthony Merry, but he saved his vitriol for Elizabeth Leathes Merry. There is no doubt that Elizabeth was a woman of presence. Margaret Bayard Smith described her as a "large, tall, well-made woman" who appeared in striking ensembles that might have been proper attire for a court but stood out in rustic Washington. Moreover, she was educated, well read, and articulate. Margaret also called her "masculine," meaning that she was "a woman of fine understanding," rivaling a man. In fact, according to Margaret, "she is so entirely the talker and actor in all companies, that her good husband passes quite unnoticed; he is plain in his appearance and called rather inferior in understanding."

In other words, Elizabeth was the kind of woman Jefferson loathed—a lady of the court who flaunted her person and her intellect and who was involved in politics. During his time in courts, he had seen women like her and no doubt had such creatures in mind when he compared American women favorably to European ladies in a letter to an American hostess: "Our good ladies, I trust, have been too wise to wrinkle their foreheads with politics. They are contented to soothe and calm the minds of their husbands returning from political debate. . . . It is a comparison of Amazons to Angels." Jefferson laid the blame for the whole affair at Elizabeth's door. He thought that Anthony would have been fine on his own, "but he is unluckily associated with one of an opposite character in every point. She has already disturbed our harmony extremely." He called her "a virago" and sniped that "in the course of a few weeks [she] had established a degree of dislike among all classes which one would have thought impossible in so short a time." In one of his communications to James Monroe, James agreed: "The manners of Mistress Merry disgust both sexes and all parties."[5]

This was a bad state of affairs. Every time Anthony Merry did not appear, as for instance, at the annual Fourth of July levee, his absence underscored Jefferson's blunder. Anthony also encouraged the other diplomats, especially the Spanish minister, to join him. Delighted at this opportunity to cause trouble, Martínez de Yrujo played off both sides, in order to see what course of behavior would be to his, and Spain's, benefit. Within a month of the Merrys' arrival, social circles in Washington were at a standstill, a critical disadvantage: in a town with little political structure, society was crucial to politics.

Perhaps more seriously, the Merry debacle stirred the ever-simmering pot of party rancor. The Federalists used Jefferson's boorish behavior to depict him as an unfit leader who ruled from "pride, whim, weakness, and malignant revenge." Republicans took their leader's side and official line, defensively blaming the Merrys, especially Elizabeth. They situated the Merry Affair in the Scottish Enlightenment movement to create new national manners; the Old World Elizabeth Merry was no republican mother. The Republicans took their revenge by trampling on her dresses and refusing to admit her to parties if she wore her "undemocratic diamonds."[6] (Of course, Jefferson did not see that the ill feeling of "all classes" toward Elizabeth was of his making.) Both sides made use of women in their campaigns. In an insult that Dolley would never forget, the Federalist press accused Dolley of having an affair with Thomas Jefferson, citing as proof the first weeks of the Madisons' arrival in Washington, when they stayed in the president's house. In an outrageous fabrication that was nonetheless typical of newspapers of the era, they also claimed that the president had pimped out Dolley and her sisters to the corps diplomatique.

No wonder the Merrys felt that America was populated by crude and quarrelsome savages. Their position as aggrieved parties tempted anyone who had a plot against the Union or a grudge against Jefferson to approach them. Sometime in 1805, Aaron Burr began plotting to seize territory either out west or in the middle of the country and create an independent nation. Hoping to get support from Great Britain, he approached Anthony Merry. Influential New Englanders who wanted to secede from the Union did as well. It is tribute to Anthony's professionalism that he did not follow up with any of these plots or use them to get his revenge on Jefferson.

But all this rancor did color the reports he sent to Great Britain. He interpreted any attempts to negotiate as just more occasions for insult. Though it is not true that the Merry Affair led directly to the War of 1812, it is true that what the Merrys saw—the bitter political attacks, the fierce newspaper war, the various plots that came their way—convinced them that the nation was inherently unstable and that Great Britain should concede nothing. In the view that they passed on to the British crown, either the republic would fall apart, or it would be taken over by another nation, in which case, present negotiations were useless.

From where Anthony and Elizabeth stood, disunion seemed inevitable, and with an expected takeover by France or Spain, it was best not to make any concessions at the present moment. Consequently, Great Britain's unwillingness to negotiate boundaries and trade policies, bolstered by this impression of national instability, did lead to the War of 1812. In addition, based on the Merrys' impression of divisiveness, when the United States finally declared war on Great Britain, the British thought they stood a good chance of negotiating a separate peace with the New England Federalists. In was in their interest, then, to extend the war as long as possible, hoping that a long conflict would force New England to secede.

Though she has left us no comment about the Merry Affair, Dolley clearly learned valuable lessons. With the newspaper attacks on her virtue and that of her sisters, Dolley understood how all the precepts about excluding ladies from the dirtiness of politics prevailed only until it was politically necessary to drag women through the mud. Jefferson had used the Merrys to make a statement about diplomacy and about Great Britain; he also used them to make a statement about women in a republic. She saw what happened to a woman who was too aristocratic.

Dolley also played her part in cleaning up the mess made of Anglo-American relations by James and Jefferson. Because Jefferson never apologized, the Merrys never dined again at the executive mansion. Instead, they used the Madison home on F Street as a substitute, so that the all-important business of diplomacy took place not at Jefferson's table but at Dolley's.

Dolley did not like Elizabeth Merry; she did not share with her the instant warmth that she enjoyed with many other women, local and diplomatic. Even after months of acquaintance, to Dolley, Elizabeth was "still the same strange [lasse?]"—"she hardly associates with any one—allways rideing on Horse back." But a professional politician does not associate exclusively with people they like, and Dolley worked hard to build a working relationship with Elizabeth, making amends for the president and smoothing things over with the locals.

On hearing Elizabeth's wish for a certain perfume, Dolley willingly gave her own Essence of Roses. Two years into the Merrys' stay, Dolley could report to sister Anna that the two were "unusialy intimate," though Elizabeth amused Dolley with "[her] airs," and "You know when she chuses she can get angry with person as well as circumstances." Still, when Dolley fell ill, Elizabeth felt close enough with her to declare herself Dolley's nurse.[7]

The "Cannons" disappeared from sight. On his next and subsequent diplomatic presentations, Jefferson was properly formal in dress and manner, and the culture of the capital drifted back to older norms. Pele mele was no more. It was clear to everyone that a new style of personal and political interaction was needed—Jefferson was right about that—but it had to be a style that was at once American while also borrowing the best Old World aspects.

Moreover, whatever the style was going to be, it had to accommodate many people with many points of view and political goals. Jefferson's social style only accommodated a narrow range of goals—his, in fact. The Merry Affair highlighted in bold relief how fragile the republic was. More than ever, unity was needed on all fronts.

5

"A Perfect Palace"
Dolley Creates the White House

DURING THE YEARS of James Madison's tenure as secretary of state, 1801–1809, he and Dolley experienced many personal changes and losses. The month before the Madisons even arrived in Washington, James lost his father, leaving his mother to run Montpelier. Anna Payne's 1804 marriage to Massachusetts (later Maine) congressman Richard Cutts would seem to be an occasion for celebration, especially as his official duties meant that the new Mrs. Cutts would be near her big sister Dolley for at least a part of every year. But to Dolley, losing her little "daughter-sister," as she called Anna, was a heavy blow, and she did not hesitate to tell her so. Even when Anna was on her honeymoon, Dolley mourned: "I continue to miss you both, & to lament a seperation from you, who could have made my happiness—."

In 1805, Dolley and James experienced one of the few separations in their marriage. In the summer, Dolley suffered from "a sad knee," which confined her to bed. It soon became clear that she needed the help of a specialist, and, accordingly, at the end of July the Madisons traveled to Philadelphia to consult with the famed Dr. Physick, who immediately confined Dolley in rented lodgings for a months-long course of treatment that included bed rest and one "little incission," as Dolley reported to Anna. James remained with her until October, when he had to return for the congressional season. Dolley was well enough to travel to Washington by November, but the couple felt their comparatively short separation keenly.

It was during this time that Dolley's renewal of acquaintance with the Quakers gave her "terrors." Being without James in a city with such bad associations, faced with a serious incapacitation, depressed Dolley. Still, she hid these concerns from her husband, and her letters to him stressed how much she loved him: "Think of thy wife! who thinks and dreams of thee!" James responded in loving kind to his "dearest" wife. He also passed along political information, answering Dolley's inquiries. She had written, "I wish you would indulge me with some information respecting the war with Spain and the disagreement with England, as it is so generally expected here that I am at a loss what to surmise."

Dolley had always had a gift for using spaces to make connections with people, and though she could only move from couch to bed, her sickroom soon became a central meeting place for prominent Philadelphians, as well as travelers and visitors. She created almost a satellite version of the house on F Street. The founders, even including champions of the Potomac capital, had worried that Washington City's location was too isolated. They were right, as many Americans felt no connections to the federal seat. Even in her illness, Dolley brought the capital to Philadelphia, one of the most important cities in the nation.

She kept up her relations with the French and Spanish diplomatic families. Dolley, who would become a most notable patronage player, getting government jobs for men in early Washington City, also worked to get jobs or Revolutionary War pensions for citizens who petitioned her. Even as she connected James with the people, James himself was not above reminding her that people like "Mrs. Lieper" (the wife of a wealthy tobacco merchant) needed a bit more cultivation. He also advised her how to handle those who would press her for information. After supplying her with a long, detailed answer to her query about the foreign situation, he added: "The power however of deciding questions of war and providing measures that will make or meet it, lies with Congress and that is always our answer to newsmongers."

While Dolley asked James about the situations with Spain and England, she was also a source of information. During her stay in Philadelphia, rumors swirled around Washington City that Spain had declared war on the United States. In an age in which communication was slow and journalists not trustworthy, such rumors had weight. In November, before she returned home, Dolley could report to James that the rumors were not true. During a party in Dolley's sickroom, another savvy woman, Charlotte Coates Stuart, wife of portrait painter Gilbert Stuart, had gotten a denial from the horse's mouth—the Spanish minister himself. Dolley could also cast some light on the always tense relationship between the United States and France, reporting that General Turreau, the French minister, had not impressed the wealthy and distinguished Philadelphians, and he knew it. "He says," reported Dolley, "that the Americans hate him."

Though Dolley was happy to be restored to James's arms in November 1805, her troubles were not over. Over the next two years, she had to cope with the death of two little nieces and then the death of their mother, Dolley's sister Mary. Dolley's own beloved mother also died, possibly from a stroke. This loss drove Dolley into a deep depression. Dolley confided the depth of her "deep affliction" to her best friend, Eliza Collins Lee, despairing: "Eliza, I cannot write—tho I wish to communicate every thing to you; when I trace the sad events that have occured to me, I feel as if I should die two." Troubles in Dolley's immediate family were brewing as well. Dolley's son, Payne, was proving to be a disappointing scholar, and his mother, who could never seem to say no to him, indulged his whims.[1]

In spite of it all, Dolley continued to make the F Street house a center for Washington politics. As Jefferson's second term was winding down, the focus of her work shifted, from merely supporting her husband's work with the president to working for his election. James was running not only against the Federalist opponent, Charles C. Pinckney, but also against fellow Republicans. In spite of, or perhaps because of, their dominance on the political scene, the Republican Party was splintering. James found himself also running against the vice president, George Clinton from New York, and against James Monroe, then minister to Great Britain, the choice of a Virginia faction led by John Randolph, who was motivated supposedly by his devotion to republican ideas but also opposed his Virginia neighbor out of sheer cussedness. Not only might another Republican prevail over James, but the Republican candidates might split the vote, giving the election to the Federalists.

Though there were definitely at least two parties running, during this era there were no party systems and no formal electoral machines in place. Men who ran for office proved their worth by seeming not to run for office, preferring to cast themselves as virtuous and above politics. The model for political men was Cincinnatus, an aristocrat from the ancient Roman Republic, who demonstrated his civic virtue by removing himself from politics. Only when the citizens called for him to serve did Cincinnatus leave his plow and his farm to return to power.

If an aspiring man was lucky, he had a wife who would run for him. Accordingly, in a time of no campaigns or campaign managers, the house on F Street became James's campaign headquarters and Dolley his manager. If James asserted his political virtue by declaring that he would not go to anyone's house for dinner for fear of appearing corrupt, he did not have to. Dinner was at his house.

Obviously, Dolley's entertaining was local, but even though a presidential election was a national event, the direct cultivation of congressmen was crucial. Not only were presidential candidates chosen by congressional caucus, in the early days of the US presidential elections there was a good chance that the election would end up in the House of Representatives. So when Dolley was winning over members of Congress, she was really courting votes.

Of course, the Madisons probably stood little chance with diehard Federalists, but with their entertainments they could rein in any apostate Republicans and rally their supporters. Then as now, everyone loves to back a winner, and making James the Republican among Republicans went a long way toward his success. If James could not "stand" for office, Dolley could. She stood in for her candidate, and her own personality and gracious way of entertaining all sent their own messages. The way she looked and acted assured Americans that a family of superior breeding, character, and refinement was leading them. Others, notably Jefferson, might speak of an American aristocracy; Dolley embodied it.

She impressed people with her own "virtuous" eschewal of partisan politics. As Margaret Bayard Smith remembered many years later: "In these trying times, Mrs. Madison appeared to peculiar advantage, her husband was assailed with all the violence of political animosity, and calumnies invented where facts were wanting. Amid this cruel warfare of conflicting parties, so calculated to excite angry feelings, Mrs. Madison . . . met these political assailants with a mildness, which disarmed their hostility of its individual rancor, and sometimes even converted political enemies into personal friends."

Dolley's career is a perfect illustration of the gendered dynamic of early republican politics. Because women were to be excluded from politics, they could also appear above the partisan fray, as disinterested patriots. Dolley's visibility as a unifying force had both positive and negative associations. Six months before the election, on July 4, 1808, it was to Dolley that a cavalry troop presented their colors and passed the Madison house. It was to her that they presented "an elegant standard" and a patriotic address.

But she also became the target of a smear campaign that focused less on politics and more on sex. Political power was synonymous with virile masculinity, and the fact that James Madison had never sired any children seemed to prove him politically impotent as well. It is true that the revered General Washington had also not fathered children, but no one dared say the same of him. George Washington's stature, tall and muscular, and his physical vigor embodied the masculine ideal; James's slight frame and air of ill health seemed to lend credence to the depiction of him as a sterile "dead head." A "pygmy," as one newspaper called James, "lack[ing] amorous passion," was no fit man to lead a country.

To critics, James's possible sterility was more than a function of his own coldness and lack of masculinity. For the Madisons' enemies, Dolley was at fault as well. Following the medical knowledge of the day, men were the ones who possessed sexual "heat"; if a woman went against nature and was too "hot," she could make both herself and her husband sterile. Dolley's physical robustness and appeal to the opposite sex seemed to prove that she was an unnaturally lustful woman. Not only would such a woman burn up her husband, but surely she would have to go outside the marriage to satisfy her sexual insatiability.

Outraged, New York senator Samuel Latham Mitchill wrote his wife, Catharine: "Your friend Mrs. Madison is shockingly and unfeelingly traduced in the Virginia papers." The old stories about Dolley being pimped out by Thomas Jefferson never really died, and the overheated election atmosphere revived them. Madison enemies delighted in fanning the flames, as when postmaster Gideon Granger drew more attention to the stories by ostensibly trying to refute them through a public duel. Virginian John Randolph of Roanoke, famous for his vitriol, preferred the subtler weapon of insinuation. Rumored to have knowledge of Dolley's affairs that would "make the hairs of congress stand [as] erect" as porcupine quills, Randolph purred to James Monroe: "You, my dear Sir cannot be ignorant . . . how deeply the respectability of any character may be impaired by an unfortunate matrimonial connection—I can pursue this subject no farther. It is at once too delicate and mortifying."

The Madisons tried to dispute these stories, but fighting gossip is like fighting smoke. For instance, they openly invited Congressman Samuel Hunt, one of Dolley's supposed lovers, to a family dinner. All the Madisons could do, however, was ignore the whispers and rumors whipping around the capital. Samuel Mitchill was not the only one shocked at the lengths the press and the partisans would go. Others sprang to Dolley's defense. One anonymous defender assessed that Dolley's "frankness, and patriotism, her loveliness, and her sincerity have long excited the suspicions, alarms and apprehensions" of political enemies of all stripes, including "partisans of France" and "democrats." This source bewailed that no sooner than James indicated a pro-British position, Dolley's "influence was proclaimed, her character assailed and her reputation bespattered."

Of particular pain to Dolley were stories and accusations that she had left her first husband to die alone of yellow fever. It is true that John Todd did not die in the country lodgings where he sent his family to save them from contagion. In fact, once he had ascertained that he had brought the disease with him from pestilent Philadelphia, he isolated himself over his wife's objections, according to Dolley. The stories making the rounds in 1808 had Dolley banishing him to die "in the open air," possibly hastening his death. If James's failure to procreate made him unfit for public office, then, wondered one critic, "Can a woman, who thus acted with a worthy husband, love her country, be a republican and know anything about patriotism?" No wonder Dolley's defender concluded that when it came to the American press, if a man is of the paper's party, "he is . . . the best of men; if a political opponent,— the worst of all created beings."[2] The same went for that man's wife.

Still, Dolley carried on, entertaining a company of between fifteen and twenty for dinner, even as, on occasion, she was too sick to "quit her bed." Social attendance meant political allegiance; her guests understood that by attending the Madisons' festivities, they were making a political statement. Federalists well understood the political uses of society. They chose to use the social sphere in a negative way, by boycotting parties and refusing to dine at the president's house.

In comparing James Madison to George Clinton, New York senator Samuel Latham Mitchill reported to his canny wife, Catharine: "The former gives dinners and makes generous display to the members [of Congress]. The latter lives snug in his lodgings, and keeps aloof from such captivating exhibitions." The crucial difference, Samuel told Catharine, was that James "has a wife to aid in his pretensions. The Vice-President has nothing of female succor on his side. And in these two respects Mr. M. is going greatly ahead of him."

With the field of society to themselves, it is not surprising that the Madisons prevailed. The Republicans did not splinter—the Federalist candidate, Charles Cotesworth Pinckney, won 47 electoral votes, but James won the day with 122 votes. Because runner-ups became vice president, James's former rival, George Clinton, with his six electoral votes, once again took that office.

Many were pleased that the Madisons were now the leading family of the country and the capital city. As Dolley's niece Mary Cutts put it, "What wonder then, that an event which placed Mrs. Madison in the 'White House' should give such general satisfaction and pleasure!"[3] Mary was referring to the "citizens of Washington," who would be pleased at continuing to be involved in national politics, but the Madison ascension was probably as satisfactory to the professional politicians, who welcomed the opportunities offered in the unofficial sphere of Dolley's social events.

Dolley Madison had intensified her efforts to connect and cultivate in order to ensure her husband the presidency. Luckily for the nation and the capital, she took those networks and techniques with her into the executive mansion. She built on her former success with a shift in focus. Obviously, Dolley always worked for her husband's interests, but she loved her country, and with James's election, she was able to conflate what James thought best with what was best for the country. Not everyone might agree with her, but it was true that since he was the man in charge, her efforts on his behalf were in the national interest. When it came to a practical plan for unity, however, Dolley's focus was on her own backyard.

The divisions in capital society were the nation writ small. The political climate had never been nastier, with partisan bitterness on all sides. James's election in 1808 may have truly sealed the Federalists' fate as a dying party, but if we judge from their words and actions, they were determined to take down their opponents before they left. The election of 1808 coalesced the disintegrating Republican Party into several clearly defined camps that shared a common goal: the "Old Republicans," spearheaded by fellow Virginian the vicious John Randolph of Roanoke; the New York Clintonites, led by George Clinton and his son DeWitt; and the behind-the-scene "Invisibles," made visible by, fittingly, not a politician but a newspaper editor, William Duane of the *Philadelphia Aurora*. Though all putatively of James's party, all set out to knock him off his throne.

Political ideology was not the only thing that further divided Congress. In this era, Americans worried about the alienating effects of "regionalism" (later in the century, they would call it "sectionalism"), which the Congress modeled in bold relief. To be sure, all these elected and appointed individuals were the elites of their areas, but even class was no guarantee of solidarity. In a culture that believed in "blood," not only along racial lines but also along regional ones, "hot-blooded" aristocratic Virginians looked down on prosperous "cold" New Englanders, and vice versa. Election to political office from rural regions brought new and surprising characters into official society.

With both shock and amusement, European visitors and diplomats, as well as American elites in the capital, related stories about men out of their element. Rural farmers-turned-politicians from New Hampshire and Vermont, along with rough-and-tumble men from the new western territories, found Washington ways confounding. According to a letter to her sister Jane, Margaret Bayard Smith could hardly contain her astonishment when confronted with two venerable senators, one a judge, who had never seen a piano. They touched the instrument "over and over," and expressed amazement when daughter Susan Smith lifted the lid. "'Dear me,' said the judge, 'How pretty those white and red things jump up and down, dear me what a parcel of wire.'" According to Margaret, they could not fathom the idea of reading music, "supposing all Susan's sweet melody was drawn by chance or random with this strange thing." Margaret cautioned Jane: "Do not think now these good men are fools, far from it, they are very sensible men and useful citizens, but they have lived in the back woods thats all."

Some stories focused on the lack of social graces involving dining and food. Men familiar with beer and cider drunk in log cabins spit out champagne and crawfish onto Turkish carpets. Faced with a lean cut of mutton, a former butcher at the president's table appalled his fellow dinner guests by declaring that he would have never dared sell the president such a miserable cut of meat. At a dinner given for an American cabinet member and his wife, the British minister's wife, Mary Bagot, could not restrain her curiosity when she saw a female guest elbow-deep in the salad bowl. "'My dear Mrs. S—what can you be doing?'" The American guest showed no shame as she promptly replied, 'Only rollicking for an onion, my lady!' (It must be stated that Mary Bagot lived for these stories, dubbing herself an "Exile in Yankeeland.")

No doubt people shared these stories because of their humorous elements. When a local tavern keeper was caught relieving himself in the fireplace of British legation secretary Augustus John Foster, the secretary merely laughed. But the elite Federalists and Washingtonians took these tales seriously, as an indicator of darker forces. Surely the movement toward "democracy" was going too far if it brought such boors to the height of national power.

Established and educated easterners looked on their western compatriots almost as through they were foreigners. They characterized them as "Irish," even though only one of the group had been born in Ireland, because they were (according to the elites) ignorant, quarrelsome, and drunk. More and more, the elite from all regions wondered if they had anything in common with such men.

"Disunion" was always a threat to the young republic. European transplant and elite gentry woman Rosalie Stier Calvert was a sophisticated and often acerbic political observer. She spoke for many with her assumption: "My opinion is that a separate republic of the northern states will be formed, and after a lot of turmoil, a monarchy in the south."[4] In this atmosphere, capital culture clash was a cautionary tale. James attempted to overcome regionalism in his appointments, saddling himself with a weak, if diverse, cabinet. He had few of the presidential carrots and sticks available today in order to lead a rebellious and divided Congress. His only choice was to unify them. Given his own personal limitations, his reticence and lack of charisma, the job of unity fell to Dolley.

The first thing Dolley did was to create a place where everyone could come together. Dolley is famous for "redecorating" the president's house, a task seen by later generations as a properly traditionally feminine act, an exercise in personal taste, featuring that most female of activities, shopping. But this assumption is wrong on two counts. First, what Dolley and her colleague, architect Henry Latrobe, did was more of a restructuring than a mere redecoration. Second, the restructuring of the executive mansion belongs more in the tradition of castle building and gentry home construction than modern ideas of home renovation that creates private spaces for a family.

The construction of such homes for public power was largely the province of men, such as George Washington and Thomas Jefferson, who built the iconic Mount Vernon and Monticello, respectively. That James Madison turned this project over to Dolley is a demonstration of his trust in her expertise. Moreover, such houses, if well done, can have tremendous psychological power, and, indeed, Dolley's manifestation of the president's house soon acquired a nickname—"The White House"—and became a symbol of the capital city.

James so prioritized this task that he engaged Henry Latrobe even before he was officially inaugurated. He chose Latrobe because he had worked on the "President's Palace," as it was called, under Jefferson. In addition, Latrobe's wife, Mary, had known James's "very excellent and amiable wife from a child." Even the fractious Congress recognized something had to be done with the shabby and unfurnished mansion (Jefferson had left with the furniture he had brought from Monticello) and came together to pass a $20,000 appropriation for the task. In order to get the social calendar up and running as quickly as possible, Dolley and Henry concentrated on three public rooms: a large drawing room for big parties (known as the Oval Room), a smaller parlor for more intimate gatherings, and the presidential dining room.

In the beginning, Henry did not spend much time in Washington. He and his wife, Dolley's childhood friend Mary Hazelhurst Latrobe, lived in Philadelphia. As it happened, most of the early stages of the project involved shopping, and, happily, Philadelphia was one of the most (if not the most) cosmopolitan cities in America and a major seaport for imports, offering the widest selection of the kinds of luxury goods needed for the first house of the land. Henry also traveled to New York and to Baltimore, where he hired the famed Finlay furniture makers to construct the presidential furniture.

In making their choices about furniture and objects, Dolley and Henry faced a serious challenge. They could not merely construct the finest decor that money could buy. There were political considerations. Dolley and Henry knew their audiences would be composed of American and European visitors who saw lavishness as a proper indicator of authority. Americans may have fought a revolution against all things regal, but monarchy and aristocracy still remained their vocabulary of power. These Americans, like others in Western Europe, believed in "rank," that some people were born better and should rule over others. Luxurious possessions and the knowledge of how to use them signaled the kind of refinement that distinguished those "betters." Superior things might make superior rulers or the other way around, but the connection was obvious in American minds.

Members of the "aristocratic" Federalist Party, who were already using the issue of slavery to differentiate themselves from Southerners, would also need the reassurance that the decadent, slaveholding Virginians could rise above the barbarity of plantation life and enter into the elevated sphere of refinement. At the same time, old-time republicans, as well as the new "democrats," the extreme followers of Jefferson's "pure republicanism," were suspicious of any court-like shows of splendor. In the tradition of paranoid political pundits, they saw "signs" everywhere, and a White House fit for a king might well soon harbor one.

In suiting their audiences, Dolley and Henry did well. Though their final product would be the most lavishly decorated public space in the nation, whenever they could they bought American, a fact not lost on American manufacturers, who sent their products in hopes that Dolley would display them. In the Madisons' own house in Montpelier, the art on the walls depicted a variety of topics, including classical, religious, and natural scenes; in the new White House, the art was American in theme and stressed heroes and statesmen. At Montpelier, the Madisons preferred French-style furniture and objects. But in the nation's house, the furniture not only came from the Baltimore firm of Finlay's but also boasted the US coat of arms as an embellishment. In addition, in decorative touches and motifs, Henry used Greek symbols in order to stress the relationship between the new United States and ancient Greece, the birthplace of democracy.

Even if money or ideology had been no problem, there were other obstacles that Dolley and the Latrobes (as Mary and son, Henry, were soon recruited to help) had to face. The Embargo Acts of 1807 and 1808, passed to restrict foreign trade in order to protect American interests meant that some items could "not be had for Love or Money," in Mary's words. "Real gold Perl" or "gold thread of any kind" could not be found, even in Philadelphia; Dolley wanted red silk damask for her curtains, but she had to settle for velvet. (Henry thought the heavy red curtains would "ruin" the effect of his gray Oval Room, but they became a famous and much noted feature, bringing warmth and light into the pale room.) The Latrobe family turned into intrepid shoppers, hunting out everything fine that could "be had" and making compromises when they could not find the best. The White House would have blue and white "India Stone china," despaired Mary: "We must have taken this, or none." She obtained coffee cups and saucers at a good price— fifteen dollars a dozen, with teacups only ten dollars for twelve.

Every grand house needed a formal tea set, and Mary found some "beautiful french china" in pea green with gilt edges and bought the set, even at the high cost of seventy dollars. Many Americans had never seen forks and, indeed, were suspicious of such frippery, but Henry and Mary bought forks and other cutlery with ivory handles. Henry found red, lacquered serving trays, "the largest I have ever seen," perfect for serving large crowds. He bought the newest Argand lamps, which gave off seven times the amount of light cast by candles, and they, along with costly wax candles for atmosphere, would dispense ample amounts of clean, pure light. To Americans used to the sputter and smell of tallow candles, they would dazzle.

The yellow parlor was finished first. Though the Oval Room would take months to finish, Dolley held her first event, called a "drawing room," in the parlor on May 31, 1809. Almost everyone marveled at the "very latest . . . style" of "Mrs. Madison's parlor," done in sunflower yellow. Trimmed with yellow silk fringe, yellow silk damask framed the windows and was hung in swag valances all along the top of the room. The fireplace board depicted a rising sun (a popular political metaphor) in the same yellow fabric. The furniture was also upholstered in yellow, and a pianoforte and guitar signaled sophistication and cultured leisure. Though this room hosted large gatherings in lieu of the unfinished Oval Room, eventually this would be the place where Dolley held intimate events, receiving calls from locals and officials, ladies of the town, and legislators.

With one success behind them, Dolley and Henry turned to the rest of their projects. The dining room did not call for much renovation, but there was one major issue that Henry mediated. Dolley wanted the large Stuart painting of George Washington hung in her parlor, but James wanted it in the dining room to begin a presidential portrait gallery. Henry sided with James, apologizing to Dolley for "counteract[ing] . . . any wish of yours," but "the dining room is properly the picture room."[5] Dolley conceded, substituting the picture of General Washington with a portrait of herself.

As anyone who has ever refurbished a house knows, there is always drama and setbacks. It is during one of these that Dolley uncharacteristically revealed some of her own political techniques and philosophy. Generally, Dolley was a woman of action, not words. Not for her the long political disquisitions and theories that pepper the letters between the men of the founding generation. Her work toward unity is discerned from what she did and the comments left by others. Part of this was deliberate. Dolley posed as "merely" a gracious lady with no interest in politics, even as she politicked like a pro. But in this case, when Henry responded to rumors of Dolley's dissatisfaction with his work, Dolley showed a little of the process behind the pose.

As Henry was rushing around getting ready to debut the Oval Room, one of his workers, Mrs. Sweeney, flatly refused an order from him, telling the distressed architect that he had no authority over her, as Dolley was, as Henry related to Dolley, "so displeased with my conduct especially with my long absence in February and April that you intended that I should do nothing more for you." To make matters worse, Henry also received two anonymous letters making the same accusations of neglect.

Henry wrote to his friend and patron, at once dismissing Mrs. Sweeney's story, which was "completely contradicted by yourself in the whole of your conduct towards me," while justifying himself regarding the charges. Henry *had* been gone for months at a time, but he was on official business, buying things for their house project. Dolley replied soothingly: "Incredulous, indeed must be the ear that receives, without belief the 'Varnished tale'"—that is, the lie. Her theory was that Mrs. Sweeney was disgruntled because Dolley had not given her much responsibility. After all, the lady in question was a fashionable Georgetown upholsterer, and Henry was asking her to wash curtains! Dolley deemed Mrs. Sweeney "a woman of many words," and told Henry that she would not dream of talking "to her, or before her," not even acknowledging Mrs. Sweeney's opinion.

She gently reproved Henry for his lack of faith in her, as evidenced by her conduct toward him and her "affection for Mrs. Latrobe," which "would in itself prevent my doing injustice to her Husband." Dolley dismissed the various charges made against him and reassured him: "tho' our enemies may strive to throw around me ungrateful appearances I shall take a pleasure in counteracting their designs." Dolley advised him, from lessons she had learned painfully, that when it came to politics, "most happy would it be, for you, could you listen *without* emotion" to lies that were "framed but to play, on your sensibility."

The Oval Room debuted for the 1810 New Year's Day reception, stunning visitors. The effect of the lights was enhanced by the largest mirrors most Americans had ever seen, as well as copious amounts of silver objects. The red velvet curtains "blaze[d]," according to one visitor, contrasting with the cream wallpaper and woodwork shadowed in blue and gray to imitate marble. These interiors spoke of European opulence, but the furnishings made them American. "The President's house is a perfect palace," exclaimed one visitor, but it was a republican one.[6]

Dolley and Henry had succeeded in their efforts to impress, but it was the use to which these lavish rooms were put, and the atmosphere set by the leading lady, that transcended mere conspicuous consumption. The renovation effectively expressed Dolley and Henry's aims: they did not expend much energy or money on the private chambers but instead restructured the space into several large, sumptuous public rooms. Before Dolley's version of the White House, there was no one space in a public building or a private home in the whole area that could accommodate all the members of the federal government, let alone their families and the locals.

For politics to happen, two spheres of activity are needed. The official sphere is that of the product of politics—the declaration, the legislation, the press release. The unofficial sphere is what many call "behind the scenes," where the process of politicking, lobbying, persuading, etc., goes on. Unofficial spheres develop at social events and in private places, such as homes. The unofficial sphere, then, offers opportunities for women to behave politically. They may have been excluded by their gender from the official sphere, with its overt shows of power, but as wives and hostesses, they could exert their own influence over political processes. Male figures dominate the history of official spheres; if we take the unofficial sphere seriously, women are its leading figures.

It is as this place of process that the White House mattered so much in early Washington. Surely it is significant that only in the halls of Congress, right in the center of the glare of the official spotlight, could the warring members of Congress meet. Politicians of both houses tried to implement boardinghouses as places for process, but their lodgings were small and tended to be populated with groups of like-minded men. Starting in 1809, all these men and more would gather at "Mrs. Madison's house." The capital city had found its unofficial sphere.

6

"A Place to See and Be Seen"
The Uses of the Drawing Room

DURING THE MADISON administration years, from 1809 to 1817, on Wednesday nights there was only one place to be: "Mrs. Madison's drawing rooms," as they were called. The Madisons adopted a form of European royal levees but called them "drawing rooms," which seemed less foreign while still evoking the aristocratic mystique of the British gentry. The simplest sort of weekly gathering would have been of universal interest in a town with few private residences (most of the official families lived in boardinghouses), with none able to accommodate more than a small gathering. But the Wednesday night drawing rooms were lavish, elaborate events and were held in the center of federal power—the White House, as it became known after Dolley's restructuring.

Locals, officials, diplomats, travelers, anyone in town for business or pleasure—they all came to the drawing room, and many of them described it. These detailed descriptions give a feel for the events themselves and the effects they had on participants; the best accounts were penned by politically minded observers and by the professional writers who attended. Catharine Akerly Mitchill, the wife of the New York congressman, was one such well-educated, savvy woman, with a taste for politics. In January 1811, she and husband Samuel Latham Mitchill were hosting one of their constituents, John Stevens, and his son, Robert. Undoubtedly, the high point of the Stevenses' visit was when the Mitchills took them to the 1811 New Year's Day version of the weekly drawing room.

The fun began in the anticipation. As the Mitchill party drew near the White House, they joined other excited guests. "It was really amusing to observe as we rode along, the great number of Carriages, all drawn as it were, by an irresistible impulse towards the great centre of attraction," commented Catharine. As their carriage approached the White House door, "the sound of sweet music struck our ears, and young Stevens eyes sparkled."

"Enlivening airs" of music swept the Mitchills and their guests in to the large gathering. Their host and hostess—"the two great personages"—James and Dolley stood at the center of the room, bowing and "courtesying," giving and receiving wishes for a happy new year. Catharine spoke with Dolley, who was wearing a dazzling silk robe that came up in a cape at her neck. The material of the loose-fitting garment was woven so that it changed color in the light. White satin ribbon trimmed the dress, matching Dolley's white satin turban, which sported a flower in the front.

Catharine then set off through the rooms "to take a peep at the company, and spy out my acquaintance." She found herself mingling with "a number of dignified characters, both civil and military . . . in short almost every important person in Washington and Georgetown, both male and female." No wonder Catharine characterized the drawing room as the place "to see and be seen." As she made her way around the rooms, she met more of her constituents, including famed New York writer Washington Irving.

Irving had traveled to Washington with the express purpose of trying to secure a position as secretary to the American minister to France. Tellingly, his strategy was to cultivate Dolley Madison, though before his trip to the capital, he had never met her. By 1811, Dolley's influence over such appointments was well known. Though he had arrived in town after a long journey only that day, he "swore by the gods I would be there . . . I mounted with a stout heart to my room, resolved to put on my pease-blossoms and silk stockings, gird up my loins, and sally forth on my expedition." He describes emerging from "dirt and darkness into the blazing splendor of Mrs. Madison's drawing room," where he met Dolley, "a fine, portly, buxom dame who has a smile and a pleasant word for everybody."

After his introduction to the lady and the president, he happily joined Catharine Mitchill. With the band playing, she and Irving promenaded up and down the Oval Room, enjoying "considerable conversation." They may have discussed his prospects; having successfully worked with Dolley on such matters, Catharine no doubt affirmed his plan to focus on her. (Unfortunately, Washington Irving did not succeed, though a few days later he reported, "Mrs. Madison is a sworn friend of mine, and indeed all the ladies of the household and myself are great cronies." It turned out Dolley had already intended this post for her brother.)

If Robert Stevens's eyes sparkled with excitement before he entered the White House, they must have been as wide as saucers once in the throng. There he saw the most lavish and elaborate interiors he would ever have seen in his life. It is not clear from which part of New York the Stevenses hailed, but even if they had been city folk, nothing they had seen could have compared to this. And the crowds! Because this was the New Year's levee, no doubt the drawing room was more packed than usual. But a "usual" crowd could be upwards of three hundred, which is why the drawing rooms were often called "Mrs. Madison's squeezes." Accordingly, Dolley opened up the dining room and the parlor as well, so that "the company were at liberty to walk about, make new acquaintance, or chat with the old ones."

No doubt the freedom of movement at the event struck Robert Stevens. The ceremonies held by the Washington and Adams administrations in Philadelphia, New York, and briefly Washington City, were staid affairs, restricted to a modest few in number. Introductions were formalized, as the women of these presidential families tried to establish an atmosphere of refinement, decorum, and muted pleasure. Both Martha Washington and Abigail Adams stood in one place as people were brought to greet them. In contrast, Dolley's crowds moved and surged, in groups of two or three or more. Most often, among the mass, one group had Dolley at its center, shifting with her as she moved to greet one and all. Dolley often wore her trademark turbans adorned with plumes, "the towering feathers . . . point[ing] her station whenever she moved," as one guest noted.

The food was mobile, too, not resting on a single sideboard or table but being carried by enslaved African Americans and hired servants. Ice cream in little dishes, cake, and other dainties were passed on those scarlet trays that Henry Latrobe had rejoiced to find. But, as Catharine warned, one had to be quick to get some of the eatables, as people could be quite aggressive in their pursuit, and the "good things will all slip away." Little side tables stationed throughout the room also held the treats, along with nuts, fruit, coffee, tea, and other party fare.

The members of the foreign delegation were no doubt splashes of colors and exoticism in the crowd. During one of the regular Wednesday night drawing rooms, White House guests spotted from a window what appeared to be "a rolling ball of burnished gold, carried with swiftness through the air by two gilt wings." It was not some sort of magical apparition but the beautiful carriage of the French minister, drawn by superb horses. When the minister himself alighted, he matched his conveyance in elaborate trim, dripping with gold lace. The most amazing part of the sight, however, was what the guests thought were wings on the carriage turned out to be, according to Sarah Gales Seaton, a guest who was the sister of one newspaper editor and wife of another, "gorgeous footmen" in brass helmets, "gilt braided skirts and splendid swords." No one had ever seen anything "so brilliant and dazzling," declared Sarah, "a meridian sun blazing full on this carriage filled with diamonds and glittering orders and gilt to the edge of the wheels." No wonder, Sarah related, that "the natives stared and rubbed their eyes to be convinced 'twas not a fairy dream."[1]

Hearing about the pleasures of the drawing room, the music, the food, the sights and sounds, and especially the gracious lady at its center, we might easily dismiss these events as merely "parties," places of amusement, and the descriptions of them as just colorful tales. But "Mrs. Madison's drawing rooms" had very specific political purposes, including the Madisons' goal of unity, and the people of the time recognized the political uses of the gatherings. When they described them, part of their reason was to evaluate what the events revealed about Dolley and James, the state of capital society, and even how the republican experiment was faring.

Taking the drawing rooms seriously highlights the role of the unofficial sphere. Every political setting needs the unofficial sphere as a place for people to propose, negotiate, and network around political business. This was especially true in Washington City, which was not only the center of the government but a city with few unofficial spaces. The very partisan bitterness of the political culture, the atmosphere of "us versus them," discouraged men of the two political parties from working with each other. Remember that, in theory at least, the "other" party was seen as a faction—and what could working with "traitors" be besides treason? With its stress on individual virtue, the foundational theory of republicanism frowned on not just working with the opposition but working together at all.

The problem was that working together got things done: a government of individuals will never work as well as a government of people collaborating and cooperating. The reason that the federal government survived under the "lone gunman" model for as long as it did was because of the nature of government work. This was an era with almost no domestic policy—the business of government was foreign relations. Consequently, congressmen could afford the luxury of scorning collaboration. They were not soliciting support for projects in their districts; there were no campaigns or organized political parties that moderns would recognize, no need to whip coalitions of colleagues to support a single candidate or a slate. There were no coattails, few carrots, and no sticks for congressmen. The most they ever worked for was to obtain federal pensions for Revolutionary War soldiers or their widows.

The reasons this state of affairs could not continue are clear in historical hindsight. In the decades right after the Madison administration, in a process that started then and accelerated after the Civil War preserved the Union, the United States emerged as a powerful government that assumed an activist role in both its own states and countries abroad. Domestic policy would become the chief function of government, even in wartime and especially when the nation was embroiled in a "domestic" war in 1861. The ruling classes needed to learn how to work together, how to give and take, how to retain their individual and collective identities as political opponents without tearing the fabric of the nation apart. They had to learn how to rule prudently when they were in power and how to be an informed dissent when they were not.

But how could that work? Everything about the new government and the new capital, even the architecture itself, mitigated against making the changes needed to help the nation grow into a modern, democratic nation-state, with a powerful presidency and a two-party system. In perhaps no other modern setting was the presence of the unofficial sphere as important than it was in early republican Washington City. And in Dolley's Washington, the drawing rooms were the premier unofficial sphere, almost the only game in town.

Catharine Mitchill's account of her own particular experience on that 1811 New Year's Day reveals in microcosm the dynamic of the unofficial sphere in action. An important aspect of the effectiveness of the drawing room was its regularity. One of the reasons the New Year's Day version was so well attended was that this rather special day was part of a larger pattern of sociability. By having these big events every week, they became an institution one could depend on. If you were a congressman with a plan, or a woman who needed a political favor from someone, you could count on the drawing room happening on that day and that everyone you knew or needed would come. It was a place with which to impress your constituents or visitors, as the Mitchills did. If the congressional season dragged on, and the city drained of all the interesting visitors, weeks might go by without any outside party or a dinner "except the drawing room, which was most magnificently attended," as one grateful congressman commented.

The clockwork regularity of the drawing room holds the clue to its institutional nature. Dolley is long reputed to be a woman who loved a party, but no one likes having to socialize on schedule. That she did shows that the uses of the parties went beyond mere amusement. Dolley held drawing rooms even when she was almost too ill to attend, "ventur[ing] down" from her sickbed. During the 1811 congressional season, Dolley sounded almost grim: "We have new Members in abundance—their wives daughters &, &, and I, never felt the entertainment of company, oppressive until now." Dolley showed the world a smiling face, implying that all she did was easy and for the sake of hospitality, but to those close to her, Dolley revealed her true feelings: "I have been engaged all the session, without an hour's leasre, & have still, a weight of cares."

In 1812, Vice President George Clinton died, but that did not stop the drawing room. A young visitor from Massachusetts, Sophia May, reported: "It was generally thought upon the Hill that there would not be any Levees altogether but they would not pay even that poor compliment to his memory." At that moment of crisis, the drawing room, with its opportunities for meetings and interactions, was of even more importance, as Dolley said: "Electioneering for his office goes on beyond description." The regularity of the drawing room—even in the face of illness and death—gave everyone a place they could count on to "see and be seen."

Bringing people together, finding a common ground, is the first step to unity. Dolley's drawing rooms were literally a bipartisan location. More like modern cocktail parties than formal receptions, people moved freely, making connections, forming and re-forming groups, and mingling. Travel observer and social critic Frances Trollope described the weekly event as having "so little attention to ceremony . . . [that] it is possible that many things may be permitted there, which would be objected to elsewhere."[2] What was possible there and not possible "elsewhere" was something people of the time did not even have a word for—bipartisanship.

The key component of access made the drawing rooms the place to be in Washington. Following general calling customs, an initial introduction to the Madisons was required for an invitation. Soon, however, Dolley's soirees became open to all, friends and enemies alike. Official families, local gentry, visitors from across the country and the globe, members of the diplomatic corps—they all met at Mrs. Madison's and were just as likely to come face-to-face with their local tailor or boardinghouse keeper.

Access to important people and to key points of decision is crucial to politics and provides important tools for implementing unity. The unofficial sphere is the best venue for access, as witness the now-professionalized capacity of lobbyists, who got their name from the practice of pitching their causes and requests outside the official halls of power, in lobbies. Of course, attendance at the drawing room gave everyone access to James Madison, who often stood, quietly greeting his arriving guests, while Dolley stood by him at the start of the events and then "worked" the room, leaving James to greet later comers. Never, before or since, has access to a president been so free. On the most obvious level, then, the Madisons promoted unity by providing access to themselves.

The genius of Dolley's drawing room, however, was that though these events centered around the Madison administration, a way to unify the party and bind people to the presidency, they offered more than that. When people praised Dolley for her "generosity," they meant more than the cakes and drinks. Dolley and her husband were generous in this gift of access. Their party guests had access to everyone in attendance.

Attendance at a drawing room offered men who knew each other the opportunity to further and deepen their working relationships. They brought together men from all the branches of government as well. Just because one man might be a Supreme Court judge and another man a senator did not mean the two might automatically know each other or see themselves connected in any way. If the architecture of Washington kept the branches of government apart, reflecting the fear of centralized power, on Wednesday nights White House architecture brought people together. Connected regularly every Wednesday night on Dolley's common ground, men could begin to build their own common ground.

Even more importantly, official men would meet their supposed enemies at the drawing rooms. With music, food, and the presence of wives and families signaling the "unofficial" atmosphere, official men could transcend the partisan political stances they felt obligated to take on the floors of Congress and in the press. No doubt much politicking was done at the drawing room by men and women, including soliciting support for legislation, floating proposals, seeking patronage, and gathering and dispensing information. Where Thomas Jefferson kept his guests on a tight leash, literally monitoring all the conversations at the table, Dolley's freewheeling atmosphere allowed many opportunities for private conversations, and people could politick as they wished.

Access also supplies information, the lifeblood of politics. During the Madisons' first term, the most compelling topic about which all were concerned was whether or not the United States was going to war, with either France or Great Britain. This was not idle curiosity on anyone's part, most especially for the diplomats who attended the drawing rooms both to seek out specific intelligence and to "read the signs."

Obviously, the diplomats, for whom socializing was part of their job description, were enthusiastic participants in the drawing room. As the previous description of the French minister demonstrates, they were not above making an entrance. Dolley used her entertainments as an extension of her own diplomatic work. When official developments made it dicey for James to "recognize" the newly arrived Chevalier de Onís from Spain, Dolley could informally recognize him with an invitation to a Wednesday night.

Conversations about war were overheard and broadcast, as they were meant to be. In 1806, Anthony Merry, at the end of his tenure as minister, was attending a last drawing room when his remark to James that "before we went to war, we ought to be very sure that no other measure of a conciliatory nature remained" sparked much political talk and maneuvering. As the person who could ask Congress for a declaration of war, James was the center of everyone's attention, as they interpreted every word and gesture, looking to discern his mind. The sight of James and new British minister Augustus John Foster "in very familiar chit-chat at the levee tonight" was enough to convince some (including Foster) that at the very least the war fires had died down and, at the most, the United States might team up with Great Britain against France.

Almost everyone reacted positively to the drawing rooms, even the political opposition. Timothy Pickering from Massachusetts might have been a rabid Federalist, but when he needed "to introduce a friend into society," the "splendor of the drawing room" provided him a perfect venue. In that era, the word "friend" stood for "political supporter," so Pickering was taking advantage of the Madisons' generosity to shore up his own political career. In more than one way, the White House entertainments rose above partisanship.

Others, especially those who had experience with European parties, scorned Dolley's efforts, but their critiques focused on aspects of the drawing room, such as the food, the guests, and so forth, rather than the idea of having a social space for politics. English minister Augustus Foster, who generally approved of Dolley and her creation of the unofficial sphere, nonetheless characterized the drawing rooms as a place where "anyone might go . . . the dirtier the better." Alexander Dick, a member of the British legation, was not impressed with what seemed to him to be merely an unruly crowd with only "tea Coffee, Ice Creams Cakes & refreshments" being the sum of "the entertainment." Like Foster, Mary Bagot, the self-proclaimed "Exile in Yankeeland," also complained about the quality and personal hygiene of the attendees: "The men—many of whom come in boots and perfectly undone and with dirty hands and dirty linen—stand mostly talking with each other in the middle of the rooms. Tea and coffee and afterwards cold punch with glasses of Madeira and cakes are handed round, and by ten o'clock everyone is dispersed."

Mary Bagot's mention of boots sounds a familiar theme in the criticisms of Dolley's "squeezes." Reflecting her style choices for the house, in her drawing rooms Dolley mixed the lure of old-fashioned aristocracy—the decor, the food, the music, her own queen-like self—with a new American style that stressed, if not a social equality, a kind of human equality. When this idea of human equality expressed itself politically, it would be called "democracy," and as the decades went by, it would be seized on by women of all races and classes and men of color in their attempts to enter the polity.

She was criticized from both sides for her attempts to find a common ground. For some vigilant Republicans, Dolley introduced what the *Alexandria Gazette* called "extravagant imitations of a royal court." Such events turned pure republican Americans into courtiers who, like their continental counterparts, would "bow and cringe, and dangle and play the parasite." According to these critics, it was by means of the "levees" (using the more courtly and sinister term) that the president seduced Congress into declaring war.

On the other side, Federalists and more fastidious members of the ruling classes thought the drawing rooms were accelerating a dangerous trend toward democracy. Using the word "Democratic" in a disparaging way, Rosalie Stier Calvert predicted that under the Madisons the more refined version of republicanism was on the way out, with dire consequences: "If the Democratic party continues to rule, a dissolution of the Union will be the result sooner or later." Rosalie enjoyed pointing out how "common," meaning vulgar and ordinary, Dolley was in spite of her lavish clothes; Rosalie mocked her by calling her "Queen Dolla lolla."

Dolley's critics often couched their fears of the unwashed hordes as Mary Bagot did, focusing on the fact that men who did not know any better came to the executive mansion in rough boots—footwear suited for labor or at least the outside world. Gentlemen of refinement would wear more formal shoes indoors and at a presidential reception. The Baltimore *Whig* tried to present the popular president's wife as a closet Federalist, claiming that she actually forbid a man wearing boots from her drawing room, a charge indignantly denied. To the contrary, Jonathan Roberts, a rigorous Republican from Massachusetts, went in his leather boots and suffered no enmity. He asserted that by allowing his boots to be on her carpet, "Mrs. Madison I understand has unequivocally declar'd she is a democrat tho the world have strong doubts about it."

It is telling that those who caviled and criticized the drawing rooms still went. Contempt for the refreshments aside, Alexander Dick admitted that "in a place like Washington where there are Scarcely any public places at all, Such a Meeting Seems to be much relished, & then there is the honor of Seeing the President & his Lady & other Public characters."[3] The parties and the opportunities they offered were indispensable to Washington business.

On occasion, the Madisons' political opponents tried to co-opt the social and political power of Dolley's soirées for themselves. Typically, they tried to do so not in a positive way—by offering up their own social agenda—but in a negative one. Prior to the election of 1812, when James was "running" for reelection, the Federalists decided to boycott Dolley's drawing rooms en masse, as a visible show of solidarity against James. The Republicans retaliated, making their statement with their presence, flooding the White House "squeezes."

Dolley regarded the Federalists' boycott, and another similar action by DeWitt Clinton supporters, as attempts to "break us." But the drawing room had such a powerful dynamic of its own that only a short while later, Dolley could smugly relate that "such a rallying of our party had alarm'd [the Federalists] into a *return*." The Wednesday night drawing rooms were where the political action was, and the Federalists could not afford to miss it. New Hampshire congressman Republican John A. Harper noted with relish that nothing in the entire congressional session had so distressed and mortified the Federalists as "finding that the

Republicans, in consequence of their [the Federalists'] conduct, paid their respects to Mr. Madison almost to a man."[4]

Perhaps the most important effect of these weekly gatherings was the subtlest, illustrated by the presence of both Federalists and Republicans. As part of their eschewal of all things monarchical, the early founders deliberately downplayed the role of ritual and ceremony in the governmental structure. For them, the ritualized shows of pomp employed by the monarchy, whether a coronation or a simple procession through the streets, were a means to display and amass absolute political power to and from a credulous and oppressed people. English and European countries had state churches, and the deliberate mixing of state and religious rituals blurred the line between the sacred and the secular, to the benefit of the state.

This aversion to allying the power of religion with state power, expressed through religious ceremonies, is part of the reason the founders were so eager to separate church and state. In their eagerness to purify the state, however, the founding generation did not consider the role of ceremony and ritual in cementing "the people" to the state, to each other, to the enterprise as a whole. Consequently, the only "ceremony" that is mentioned in the Constitution is the presidential inauguration, but it is deliberately left without details, described as scantily as possible. Paradoxically, a young nation facing an uncertain future, with no past to draw on and with a desperate need for the states to form a union, required the affirming and elevating qualities of ceremony.

In early Washington City, the drawing room functioned as ceremony or ritual. Rituals, whether they are religious in nature, such as Holy Communion, or secular, such as the Fourth of July, are episodic, and they are experienced differently from everyday life. A ritualized activity seems more special and inspires heightened emotions and sensory perceptions. The drawing room had the regularity of ritual; the sensory experiences provided the heightened reality—the visual beauty of the decor and the garb of Dolley and her female guests, the sound of live music and the excited chatter of people trying to be at their best, the exotic tastes such as ice cream and Madeira.

Rituals such as weddings and christenings mark rites of passages. The guests who passed through Dolley's drawing rooms felt that they had experienced something special that conferred on them the feeling of "insiders." The function of ritual is to supply boundaries and bonds, to confirm identities and provide structures. Like a coming-of-age ceremony, Dolley's drawing rooms brought new members into the fold. She gathered disparate members of the capital together like one big dysfunctional family, and at her drawing rooms they took the first steps toward working together.

In a political culture that framed issues in black and white, where there was no way to understand the function of an informed dissent, at Dolley's drawing rooms people could interact with everyone at their most human. If political rhetoric on both sides painted the opposition as the embodiment of evil, the reality of the drawing rooms made such characterizations hard to sustain. Women in political families forged social relationships across the aisle that neutralized the acid partisanship. They invited women of the "other party" to engage in social events, dispense charity, or even collaborate on getting a job for a worthy candidate. For the men, seeing a male political enemy with his family, getting to know his female kin apart from the overheated atmosphere of politics, played its part in showing that even though someone disagreed on an ideology or an issue, they still could have the public good at heart.

Slowly, under Dolley's eye, this motley group of former colonists was constructing a ruling class and forging the tools for the bipartisanship that the official men did not recognize but would shortly need. When, in a decade or so, it became clear that theirs was to be a two-party system, the structure laid out first in Dolley's drawing rooms, and then in the unofficial spheres of her imitators, could rise to meet the challenge. Washington City and the nation would need the constancy of rituals to ease the transition to democracy and to change, even as the rituals supplied the feeling of stability.

Of course, Dolley could have not foreseen all of these ramifications of the drawing room, in the same way that in setting up the Constitution, the founders could not have foreseen that it would function as a springboard for the greatest experiment in human freedom in history. The way to assess her efforts is, as the efforts of the founders are assessed, to determine her intention at the time. The founding men did not know that bipartisanship would be the hallmark of the system; they did not even have a word for it. Dolley did not have a word, either, but somehow, in a culture that mitigated against it, she knew to bring people together, and that working together would be the salvation of the system.

By mixing elements of the old court ways with the American trend toward democracy, Dolley created a "new-fashioned" democracy, one that changed the course of the republican experiment. By, on the one hand, insisting that ladies curtsey to the president and, on the other, curtseying back to everyone, Dolley transmuted republicanism through court culture, adapting to the nation's peculiar needs. By mingling "the Minister from Russia and the underclerks of the post office," Dolley offered a social solution to the central problem of republican politics; namely, how to make the federal government and nation cohere without an absolute power such as a king. She showed that nations do not need force for unity. The very act of unifying citizens on their own terms would result in the surest form of national unity. One step on the way to nationhood is when the people of the new entity can imagine themselves as held together in a common enterprise. In a small but significant way, Dolley's guests, looking around her rooms, could not just imagine but see their community forming before their eyes.

At the beginning and end of Catharine's account there is Dolley, reflecting the centrality of Dolley to the drawing room. Every evening has its end, and when the Mitchills and Stevenses took their leave, Catharine had a few more words with Dolley: "I observed to her that she ought to rejoice when we were all gone, for then she must be fatigued standing so long." But Dolley surprised Catharine by declaring that "she was not in the least fatigued, and that she regretted us going away so early." This was no mere social nicety to Catharine's sharp ears: "I believed she spoke the real sentiments of her heart, for I never saw a Lady who enjoyed society more than she does. The more she had round her the happier she appears to be."[5] The feeling was reciprocal. Dolley's Washington was happy to be around her.

7

The "Queen of Hearts"
Dolley's Public Persona

F OR EVERY DESCRIPTION of a Dolley Madison drawing room, there is a description of Dolley herself. People were fascinated by her, drawn by a combination of her physicality, personality, and political power. Her physical persona was always the first thing people discussed, but they quickly discerned the woman underneath her glamorous clothing. In the parlance of the time, they lauded Dolley for her "desire to please, and a willingness to be pleased," but that assessment is too passive. Her charm had more force and focus than being merely pleasing. Dolley put her persona to political use, to provide unity within a system that worked against it. Even though the people of her culture did not recognize or approve of "petticoat politicking," and her supporters would not insult her by impugning political motives to her actions, people's reactions to her, both positive and negative, reveal that they considered her a powerful friend or enemy.

Generally, the descriptions of Dolley that pepper the letters and newspaper reports of the early republic have been regarded by historians as just a form of "color commentary," not the least because they are so colorful. Men and women reported back home on what Dolley wore, what she served, how she moved, and how she treated people. But these descriptions are not mere "celebrity mentions." The people who regarded Dolley so minutely—whether members of the ruling elite or ordinary Americans and Europeans invested in the republican experiment—

were looking for signs and significance in how she looked and how she behaved.

This focus on the body of the ruler has long roots in Western court culture. In English and European courts, the ruler's body and its capacities, especially when it came to fighting and birth, were regarded as an extension or part of public policy. Loyal courtiers were rewarded with offices involving personal contact with royals, whether as ladies-in-waiting or gentlemen of the bedchamber.

After the American Revolution, at a time of flux and change, with few real political structures in place, the new Americans focused on the persons of their leaders, especially George Washington. President Washington could be merely standing on the steps, and people read "inner majesty and grace" into the figure standing "erect, serene, majestic." What they were looking for, and found in their Washington, was reassurance of the man's character and his capacity for "civic duty and moral grandeur."[1]

In the early republic, people transferred this evaluative capacity to Dolley. To them, Dolley symbolized the "heart" of the real Madison administration, but also its true character. This symbolizing capacity by women had its own long history, and Dolley was surely aware of her function. In political theory, the "charismatic figure" is a person who can convey abstract psychological and emotional messages to large groups of people. Although the psychological aspect is important to any political milieu, in the infant republic, the way the new Americans felt about how they were ruled was key to the success and survival of the nation.

Unity was Dolley's primary message, one that was specific to her husband's goals. Supporting this goal of unity was another message that Dolley conveyed, concerning authority and national legitimacy. Ironically, Dolley's message about unity was conveyed with aristocratic tones. In important ways, the American Revolution was fought not only against a king, with the absolute power attendant on such a being, but also against everything that monarchy stood for, including court life. Republicanism, especially as articulated by men such as John Adams, proudly trumpeted the virtue of manly American simplicity over the effeminate (but not necessarily female) aristocratic corruption of the

Old World, as exemplified by the royal courtier with his powdered wig and silk handkerchief. In Royall Tyler's *The Contrast*, the first produced play written by an American, the hero is Colonel Henry Manly, an exemplar of sound republican simplicity; his foil, Mr. Billy Dimple, is a simpering Anglophilic fop.

But the fires of revolution had not even died down when the ruling men began to worry, in the absence of an absolute power, how they could assert their authority over the mass of largely uneducated white men. They did not worry about authority over white women, slaves, or people of color, assuming that white men had their authority over their households in place. White male citizens, the foundation of the republic, were also its greatest threat. In a twist of poetic justice, the founding men discovered, even as they were putting the new nation together, that they might actually need the trappings of authoritarian aristocracy in order to command the people's respect.

The monarchical trappings of the Old World were the only vocabulary of power these former colonists knew, and as time passed, they began to co-opt some of these symbols of the aristocracy in order to reassure "the people" that the right kind of people were ruling them. So after the Revolution, in a breathtaking about-face, the formerly rabidly antimonarchical John Adams suddenly started arguing for bestowing titles on lawmakers, following the example of the British House of Lords. He even wanted to call the president "His Majesty" or "His High Mightiness." Newly elected President Washington found himself wondering how many pairs of matched horses pulling his carriage through the streets could convey the proper sense of authority to onlookers without becoming too unrepublican.

This was a tricky balance to achieve—how much was too much? How would the new ruling classes use the old vocabulary of aristocracy to convey the legitimacy of the national experiment without tipping over into monarchical corruption? Perhaps the Federalists, such as Washington and John Adams, would have freely brought back aristocratic practices, but a number of Americans, the ones who would be followers of Thomas Jefferson, kept a sharp eye out for "encroaching aristocracy," as they would have seen it. These men wanted nothing to do with the Old World.

As it turned out, in each instance the balance of "aristocracy/democracy" came down on one side or the other in different ways. In the case of Adams's proposal, titles were rejected, and the chief executive became "Mr. President." For his part, President Washington decided that three pairs, six horses in all, struck the right note of authority without going overboard. One of the ways this tension played out, as issues of power often do, was on the field of gender. In the end, the women of the ruling elite were given the task of conveying the aristocratic message to the masses. Because they were "private" and not elected officials, paradoxically, women had more latitude. So while George became "Mr. President," Martha became "Lady Washington," and the new Americans could project their own longings for an aristocratic ruler onto her. With his wife imparting the superiority aristocracy endowed, George Washington was safe to toe the republican line.

Thus when Dolley set out to create her persona, she was not the first woman charged to embody the elite, but as Dolley tended to do, she did it bigger and better than anyone else. In creating her public persona, one in contrast with her husband, Dolley raised the stakes on this dilemma, and while for the most part she was widely hailed for her creation of a republican queen, her choice was not without backlash.

The most obvious aspect of Dolley's public persona was the most visible—her clothing. The Madisons allocated a great deal of their resources to Dolley's wardrobe, and not a friend or family member could travel to an American or European city without Dolley asking them to shop for her. Though accounts exist of Dolley still wearing Quaker garb for her daily duties, she created a dramatic style for her public appearances. While Dolley was avidly au courant with European court styles, she did not simply adopt them. Dolley adapted European styles to suit the practical American character.

Empire dresses were the style during her Washington tenure. These were high-waisted dresses so flimsy that when the Europeanized Elizabeth Patterson Bonaparte appeared in one in Washington, it was reported that she was "nude." So Dolley would wear a white Empire-waisted gown, but one that was made of a more substantial material and, except for its low cut, modest. The Empire style was particularly suitable for Dolley's purposes, as the trend was modeled on ancient Greek styles, recalling the Greek tradition of democracy. Much as Dolley and Henry deliberately invoked the birthplace of democracy in their architectural embellishments, Dolley fashioned herself along classical lines. Tall and well built, wearing the new styles with her dark curls in a neoclassical chignon, Dolley looked every inch the Greek goddess.

Nor was her style an imitation of what passed for "court dress" on the Continent or across the pond. The clothes courtiers wore were very elaborate, specifically styled, and spectacularly cumbersome. In 1809, when John Quincy Adams and Louisa Catherine Johnson Adams served in the Russian delegation from the United States, Louisa Catherine had to be presented at court in proper dress, which included a hooped skirt of "silver tissue with a train." Over that, she wore a heavy red robe with its own train. Lace was everywhere, and added to the dress itself were jewels, fan, gloves, and, as Louisa reported, "over all this *luggage* my Fur Cloak." No wonder Louisa could barely get in and out of the carriage and that John Quincy and the other American men burst out laughing at the outlandish figure she cut.

In contrast, Dolley valued ease of movement at her soirées and could not be rendered immobile by traditional court dress. Dolley's style was almost an interpretation of what American court dress might be. If nothing else, Dolley's ensembles marked her as "elevated," above even what a wealthy woman would wear. Wife of a Massachusetts representative, Mary Boardman Crowninshield hailed from Salem, Massachusetts, one of the richest seaport cities on the coast and the entrepôt for luxurious items from around the world. But even she was floored by Dolley's dress material: yellow satin "embroidered all over with sprigs of butterflies, not two alike."

Indeed, some of Dolley's outfits bordered on the fantastical. Frances Few, the niece of Albert and Hannah Nicholson Gallatin, described Dolley's "brick coloured silk" dress, with two-yard-long, white-trimmed train and cap decorated with a "large bunch of [calico] flowers" as "Most preposterous." But if her ensembles seemed a bit over the top, it is important to remember that Dolley was not trying merely to be the best-dressed woman in the room. Even as Dolley rejected real court dress, she was trying to answer Americans' longing for what they might imagine a royal lady would look like.

It is important to acknowledge the effects that Dolley's clothes had on ordinary Americans, including high-ranking government officials who often came from very rural areas. To them, this woman seemed almost otherworldly in her elegance. Ordinary Americans were used to clothes in natural colors that came from the fabrics themselves, such as linen. If ordinary clothes had any color, it originated from the dull browns and greens of vegetable dyes. Standard dyeing practices could not produce "pure" hues very easily; white in particular was difficult to achieve, but so was a deep true black.

Even if one could use vegetable dyes to create a multicolored garment, those dyes were not colorfast. But by the time Dolley came to the White House, new dyeing techniques were made available to the upper classes that made longer lasting, bright, pure, vivid colors. Dolley would not be the only one who went a little crazy with contrasting hues that seem garish to modern eyes. The many descriptions of Dolley's ensembles demonstrate her use of these colors, as well as pure white and dramatic black.

The textures of ordinary clothing were also rough, reflecting both the coarseness of the fiber and simple weaving methods. Many everyday garments were made at home. In contrast, Dolley's dresses were made of finely woven materials, whose smooth, shiny surfaces reflected light and made the colors shimmer. Dolley used luxurious materials such as ermine, swansdown, and lace; she wore turbans and carried muffs and fans—all to create an unforgettable figure.

Indeed, her use of the turban is an example of the power of her influence. Dolley did not invent the turban for fashionable use; women of a certain age on both sides of the Atlantic were wearing them at that time. But the way Dolley styled her turbans, invoking both the regal and the exotic, made them indubitably hers, and when they wore turbans, women in the United States were copying her. When Dolley fastened plumes to her turban, she was also evoking contemporary renderings of "classical" female symbols who wore caps or helmets adorned with plumes. These classical references and political implications were not lost on her audiences; one observer referenced King Henry IV of France, who wore a white plume into battle so that his troops knew where he was, describing Dolley's headdress as the "plumes of Navarre."

Even a simple day gown of white cambric (a lightweight, plain-weave cloth) was rendered unforgettable by the quality of workmanship and accessories. One such gown boasted a ruffle around the bottom and tiny buttons with elaborately embroidered buttonholes the entire length of the dress. It was harmonized with a close-fitting jacket, scarf, and gauze turban, all in the same shade of peach. Imagine the effect of one of her formal ensembles: A deep pink satin dress, trimmed with lace, with a yards-long, white velvet train lined with lavender silk. Dolley accessorized this with a wide gold belt, necklace, and bracelet and topped it off with a white velvet turban on her head, festooned with white ostrich-feather tips and embroidered with a small gold crown.

The tiny gold crown on her turban also hints at the royal message that Dolley carried. Sometimes Dolley could go a bit far, and sharp eyes were always watching. This was an age where a profusion of gold lace on the French minister's coat led Jefferson to joke that "the boys on the streets will run after him as a sight." Dolley was wearing these clothes in order to partake of the aristocratic power they conveyed, but she had to be careful. Any use of a crown motif, as embroidery on a turban or as what a shocked New England miss called a *"sparkling diadem on her head*," not only made Republicans uneasy but even shocked Federalists, who prided themselves on their commitment to republicanism. Upon seeing Dolley's crown, the young lady from Massachusetts mourned Dolley's shocking display of royalty.

Diadems and the occasional "silver headdress . . . in the form of a crown" aside, jewelry was an important element in Dolley's ensembles, an essential part of the vocabulary of power.[2] Again, like clothes, it is easy to see earrings, brooches, and necklaces as "mere" fashion, expressions of a personal aesthetic and taste. But like the outfits they adorned, Dolley's jewels also conveyed aristocratic messages, both signaling the superiority of the wearer and tying her to ancient lineages. In important ways, jewels not only carried historical and family pedigrees (and were often recognized and named), but also acted like the medals on a military officer, identifying the wearer as someone of importance.

In European and British courts, the standard jewel was the diamond. Though Dolley wore many colored stones, she tended to avoid diamonds, precisely because they seemed too aristocratic. No doubt she remembered Mrs. Merry being rudely asked to remove her "undemocratic diamonds" before an event. Rather, Dolley favored pearls, which she famously wore to the first presidential inaugural ball, sponsored by the locals and held in her honor. Pure white pearls seemed more refined and modest—a more American choice.

"Clothes make the man," as the saying goes, but the people of Washington City did not only look at Dolley's clothes for indications of her superior nature. They looked for the signs that her persona reflected an inner grace and regalness. People attuned to royal standards understood this woman to be "Queen Dolley," as she was widely hailed, because of the way she held herself and how she moved. They called this capacity "mien," or bearing, and the standards for how a ruler commanded space came from European courts. Bearing was precisely what observers noted when they analyzed how George Washington stood on the steps, and that standard was what they brought to their dissection of Dolley.

The most favorable descriptions of Washington came when he stood; even in his lifetime, he seemed to be posing for statues. But Dolley's descriptors focused on her in action, as suited her own personality (in contrast to the stolid Washington) and her modus operandi. When people described Dolley in motion, they invoked goddesses— "stately and Minerva-like"—or royalty—"with the grace and dignity of a Queen." Passing through crowded rooms, like a queen in satin and silk, displaying her pearls and silver, Dolley was asserting her and, by extension, her husband's right to their place as the nation's leaders. Political foes and supporters alike understood this and evaluated her performance accordingly.

As she assumed the head of national society as the president's wife, Dolley constructed a lavish persona, using clothes and jewelry in ways that might seem almost outlandish but were also impressive and dazzling. Still, Sarah Gales Seaton echoed many when she followed a description of one of Dolley's extravagant ensembles with this reassurance: "'Tis here the woman who adorns the dress, and not the dress that beautifies the woman." The secret of her success, many decided, lay in her inner, rather than her outer, beauty.

The most important aspect of the Dolley persona was more than skin deep. To observers, it was who she was inside, as indicated by how she behaved and how she treated others. Story after story told of Dolley's effect on people; firsthand witnesses related with some relief how she had charmed them or put them at their ease in terrifying social situations. When young South Carolinian William Campbell Preston arrived for a Wednesday night drawing room knowing no one, he felt quite shy and overwhelmed. He was not put at ease by James Madison, who, though William had been introduced to him as a distant relative, had "an abstracted air and pale countenance, but little flow of courtesy." William stood, feeling out of place, when Dolley caught his eye. She walked right up to the stranger and said, "Are you William Campbell Preston, son of my old friend and most beloved kinswoman, Sally Campbell?" Dazed by the splendid woman in front of him, William agreed that he was. Dolley exclaimed over knowing him as a baby, and reintroduced him to the president as *her* relative. This time, James shook hands cordially.

Dolley did not stop there, declaring: "I stand towards [you] in the relation of a parent," and, as William remembered, with all the "easy grace and benignity which no woman in the world could have exceeded," proceeded to introduce William to all the people there, important men and reigning belles, urging all to consider him her "protégé." Recalled William: "My awkwardness and terror suddenly subsided into a romantic admiration for the magnificent woman before me." Dolley gained an admirer for life and added another person to her network, one who would go on to be a senator and the president of the University of South Carolina.

The episode so vividly recalled by William Preston illustrates Dolley's technique in action, including her exploitation of kin networks. The obsession with relations and connections was a particularly Southern one, but Dolley used it directly for political purposes. William was not clearly related to Dolley by either blood or marriage (his mother was a friend of Dolley's sister Anna), but what was important was that Dolley declared him so. This was part of a larger pattern. Dolley had circles of adopted daughters and sons, including Phoebe Morris, referred to by Dolley as "our daughter" in her correspondence with Phoebe's father, Anthony Morris, who became a secret envoy to Spain.

Because she was a woman, many have attributed her penchant for adopting protégés as evidence of the kind heart of a woman who only had one child and an unsatisfactory one at that. Payne Todd was growing up to be a spoiled young man; during the White House years, he would become a debauched one. But this practice seen as the province of a politician makes just as much sense. Dolley's "children" were all members of well-connected families. In the same way, Dolley was famed for never forgetting a name, a face, or a family pedigree. Obviously, this had a very flattering effect on people. Historians have attributed this skill as an extension of her caring nature, but her ability to recall the face and name of someone not seen for twenty years is the product of a superior intellect and a capacious memory, and she used it as a professional politician would: publicly and to political purpose.

Most descriptions of Dolley's charm and kindness mention her unifying effect on people. Certainly observers praised Dolley on her own for her "sweetness," for being "humble-minded, tolerant, and sincere," as someone who "certainly has the most agreeable way, of saying the most agreeable things." But the most astute commented on her personality in relationship to, and in its effects on, others. No matter "how great a person greeted her or how comparatively unimportant a guest, her perfect dignity and her gently gracious interest were the same to all." If she showed any preference, "it was to the modest and diffident," with the shyest of guests soon "put at ease by her affability." Catherine Akerly Mitchill, wife of New York congressman Samuel Latham Mitchill, after spending time with Dolley at events large and small, concluded: "Really, she makes herself so agreeable and by her civil & polite expressions, puts every one in such a good humour with themselves, that no one who has once seen her, can help being pleased with her, or quit her house without feeling a desire to renew their visit."[3]

But Dolley did not merely bring people together, generously offering the many kinds of access provided by her entertainments and letting them go to it. She also actively worked to enforce a code of civility that allowed people to see the best in each other. All of her life, Dolley was famed for her avoidance of contention. "To the powerful and arrogant, she would accord all their vanity exacted," Mary Cutts relayed. "She would say, it was not her place to treat them otherwise. One of her peculiarities was, never to contradict." Dolley herself advised one of her protégés, Phoebe Morris, that "to have conciliated the regard of those, by whom we are surrounded—it is a sensation, my dear girl, *worth all the pains you can take.*"

In an era that equated complete self-effacement with ladylike behavior, her contemporaries recognized these tendencies and mostly registered approval. Still, even by her culture's standards, she could be excessively ameliorating, even prompting some to suspect hypocrisy. When young Frances Few bluntly wondered that "I do not think it possible to know what her real opinions are as she is all things to all men," she was not the only one who regarded "those smiles which no doubt helped to make the dominant party adhesive in . . . her presidency" with skepticism. (It is true that Frances followed her expression of skepticism by also observing that Dolley's "face expresses nothing but good nature—it is impossible however to be with her & not be pleased." Even Frances had to concede: "There is something very fascinating about her.")

This eagerness to please might be one more result of her unsettled life as a young person; her avoidance of conflict could be traced to life with her father, clearly a difficult man. Such a life may have been stormy enough for her to learn the value of smoothing things over. Nevertheless, she did not merely sidestep conflict but actively reached out to charm and disarm. Dolley was always willing to face the lion in his den; she did more than avoid dissension—in her own way, she dissipated it.

On one hand, she set the example herself, as Jonathan Roberts commented: "By her deportment in her own house you cannot discover who is her husband's friends or foes. Her guests have no right to claim of her partiality." But she went beyond modeling, using her personality as a tool for policy: "All parties appeared [at Dolley's drawing rooms], knowing that they should all share her kind welcome and benignant smile. She felt that it was her duty to pour oil on the waters of discord and draw malcontents into the fold of her husband, and successful she was for few would oppose the partner of such a wife!"

Though Dolley would deny the use of her power to compel civility, it is clear that for all her gentle ways, people paid attention. Mary relates:

"So harmonious was her disposition, she never argued a point, if friends or relations indulged in satire or wit, in her presence, which might wound the feelings of others," Dolley would just absent herself. If her guests continued "indulg[ing] in satire or wit," Dolley's return would make them stop: "when the peculiar and welcome returning sound of her high heeled shoes gave notice of her approach all ill feeling would be forgotten or suppressed and the topic changed, so well known was her dislike to contention; for she always said 'I would rather fight with my hands than my tongue.'" Or in this case, her feet, which had the power to change the conversation.

Attendance at social events, even in the early republic, demanded that women and especially men behave themselves. But the circumstances—both the need for civil behavior and the factors that obviated it—were heightened in the capital milieu. Theirs was a particularly violent, masculine culture in which men assaulted each other not only in boardinghouses and on the public streets, but also on the floors of Congress. It is easy, social proscriptions aside, to predict that such goings-on might break out in the free-for-all of a drawing room. By her actions and presence, however, Dolley demanded emotional control.

She did not just let the events do her work; rather, Dolley was an active participant, implementing her own values into the events. Presiding over crowds had one effect, but Dolley also appreciated individual interactions. Indeed, even in crowds, as her experience with William Preston shows, often Dolley treated her large gatherings as a succession of personal encounters. Famed New York writer Washington Irving was not the only one who felt after his first drawing room that he "in ten minutes was hand in glove with half the people in the assemblage."[4] She also hosted intimate and chatty "dove parties" for the wives of female cabinet members, with gifts and treats for each, as well as the freewheeling, cocktail party–like events.

Building on her earlier work during the secretary of state years, Dolley also exploited the social practice of calling. Though she could have stayed in her sunny yellow parlor and received all the world, she used her carriage as a mobile unofficial space. She called on everyone in Washington who lived or visited there. Meeting them in their own homes bespoke a different kind of intimacy. And in a town of bad roads, no doubt Dolley was often around to give a ride to a stranded congressman, creating another occasion for connection.

In the way that Dolley and James's personalities and values dovetailed and complemented each other in their shared commitment to union, each Madison's public persona contrasted with and reinforced each other. While Dolley was all color, movement, and liveliness, James was described as slight in stature and almost colorless in public presence. Dolley was a larger-than-life figure, while he was a "very Small thin Pale visag'd man of rather a sour reserved & forbidding Countenance." One wag remarked that "he looks like a country schoolmaster, mourning over one of his pupils he's just whipped to death." Everyone hailed him as the father of the Constitution, "a Man of talents," even as they marveled that he seemed "incapable of smiling." At times he seemed lost in the crowd at his own house.

But, again, these descriptions have political functions and are not merely expressions of likes and dislikes. For all that people seemed to enjoy pointing out James's lack of charisma (Washington Irving called him "a withered little apple-John"), his lackluster presence reassured them. As with his leadership style, what seemed to be his weakness was his strength. In republican theory, power was in the hands of the people, not consolidated in an absolute ruler. The greatest fear in a republic was the appearance of a charismatic leader who could dazzle the populace into giving up power, making himself a tyrant.

In their lifetimes, the new Americans had seen this dynamic play out in a good and a bad way. They had observed the epitome of a charismatic man, the tall, powerful George Washington, who literally towered over the founding generation. A war hero, loved by all, acclaimed "Father of his Country," Washington had every opportunity to turn his popularity into power and his presidency into a lifetime monarchy. That he did not do so, instead retiring after two terms, was hailed as an event almost supernatural in virtue. On the other side, the spectacular rise of the emperor Napoleon from the chaos of the French Revolution showed the perils of a power vacuum and how a charismatic leader could exploit it. Small, reserved James Madison, standing in his plain, black breeches of good republican broadcloth, personified the "weak" leader of republican theory.

In the same way that the couple blended the extremes of republicanism and aristocracy in their presentation, such a paradox is the key to understanding Dolley's persona. She was a republican queen, combining regal presentation with an authentic interest and care for other people that seemed the essence of the best parts of democracy. It is important to see the republican queen as both authentic and a construction.

Like everyone else, Dolley Madison had her bad days. In her letters to her family, she could grumble, be depressed, and even express a great deal of hostility toward her husband's enemies. Among her papers is a reminder to herself: "Warning words of my husband: 'Be always on your guard that you become not the slave of the public nor the martyr of your friends.'" But she was also genuinely kind and warm, an extrovert who thrived on social interactions. Motivated by politics, she chose to show only that positive face to the world, building a persona rooted in her authentic self. Dolley made her personality a tool of policy in her husband's quest for political unity.

The sharpest observers charted Dolley's construction of her republican queen. Margaret Bayard Smith and Catharine Akerly Mitchill had both known Dolley from her days as the wife of the secretary of state and noted how she deliberately refined herself from a fun-loving, card-playing, eighteenth-century dame to a more reserved, poised, politic woman.

Dolley's admirer William Campbell Preston also had a glimpse behind the scenes. He noticed that upon James simply saying her name, "the lady, and on no other occasion, relaxed the deliberate and somewhat steely demeanor which always characterized her." The fact that Margaret, Catharine, and William understood that Dolley was performing does not mean they thought she was phony. They knew and loved the "real" Dolley, but they understood the need for a political person to project her real self in a way that "the people" could see and to which they could react.

Dolley may have been a queen in her presentation, but as one guest cautioned, "her demeanor is so far removed from the hauteur generally attendant on royalty, that your fancy can carry the resemblance no further than the headdress." Dolley's sincerity saved her, even for people who thought her manners excessively charming or her dress gaudy. She was a queen, but as many proclaimed, she was also a "*Queen of Hearts*," as Samuel Latham Mitchill dubbed her.[5] Together the Madisons gave the American people what they wanted—the solid national legitimacy that came from Dolley's aristocratic style and the reassuring commitment to "pure republicanism" conveyed by their uncharismatic president. They reassured all that the republic had a firm foundation. Theirs was a union for unity.

8

"Mrs. Madison's War"

Dolley's Role in the War of 1812

IN SPITE OF JAMES'S work in the official sphere and Dolley's efforts in the unofficial one, the political scene in Washington continued to deteriorate. Partly this was due to the political culture, which devalued collaboration across the aisle even within political parties, and where men took political attacks as seriously as personal ones, and fought to the death over affairs of honor. It did not help that the world outside the United States was in turmoil.

The center of the international crisis lay far from US soil. The Napoleonic wars between England and France had been raging since 1803. Great Britain's focus was on France's Napoleon, as he continued in his quest to dominate not only Great Britain but also all of Europe. Around the main event, ancillary conflicts popped up, including the Haitian rebellion and both nations' troubles with America, but they were so many flies to be swatted away. Like two bullies on a playground, Great Britain and France banged away at each other, while the other nations watched, sidelined but still involved.

The United States, however, did not see its problems with Great Britain as side issues. Some of its injuries were long-standing and festering, such as the lingering resentments around border disputes. One of the lasting results of the Merry Affair was that these issues never got resolved. Other difficulties were new, the result of the European hostilities. In their quest to best each other, both Great Britain and France tried to exploit the neutrality of US shipping.

All through the Jefferson and Madison administrations, both Great Britain and France used American ships as pawns in their war games, treating the officially neutral nation as an adversary or an ally when it suited them. For instance, in response to Napoleon's 1806 Berlin Decree, which forbade the import of British goods into countries allied with or dependent on France, in 1807 Great Britain issued fourteen Orders in Council that banned neutrals from trading with France and its allies. Though these Orders covered all neutral trading partners, the United States suffered the most. Not only were France and Great Britain its most crucial import and export designations, it could be doubly prohibited, at one instance being considered an ally of France by Great Britain or as neutral.

Jefferson and then James responded with various embargoes and acts, including the 1807 Embargo Act, the 1809 Non-Intercourse Act, and in 1810 Macon's Bill No. 2. These legislative acts, which Congress debated furiously, sought to penalize both European powers by withholding or restricting the US importation and exportation of goods, but to no avail. Put bluntly, neither France nor Britain cared about the fumings of an upstart former colony.

The necessities of war also accelerated a practice that the US citizenry found increasingly outrageous. The British Royal Navy was one of the finest in the world, but they secured their reputation by the use of extreme cruelty toward the ordinary sailor and extreme arrogance on the part of the command. One of their practices was to kidnap American seamen, claim them as deserters, and impress them into His Majesty's service. No doubt some of their victims were Englishmen fleeing from British oppression, but Americans were the majority of the victims, including Englishmen who had switched allegiance to the United States. Ordinary Americans were shocked and appalled by these crimes against their citizenry.

The European conflict and its consequences gave the Federalists and Republicans more issues to contend over, and their infighting centered around the question of whether or not to go to war with Great Britain. James did not share his thoughts on paper, but it seems that he was determined to keep the United States out of war for as long as he could.

The mood of the country, however, was for war on the grounds of "national honor." The lens through which the white male citizenry viewed shipping depredations and impressments of sailors was not that of practicality (though many Americans, especially in New England, suffered from the shipping restrictions) or even human rights. Rather, they chose to see these as affronts to their male pride. Of course, such a widespread national view was only magnified in a city of dueling congressmen.

The 1810 congressional elections dumped almost half of the older, mostly antiwar candidates out of the House, replacing them with younger, prowar candidates. As the 1812 presidential election neared, it became more certain that James could not be reelected without a declaration. But James continued to walk a delicate balance. The 1810 congressional freshmen represented a new kind of Republican. They were young, hailed from the western part of the country, and, in an audacious move, even added the newly rehabilitated term "democratic" to their names. These Democratic-Republicans included Felix Grundy of Tennessee and John C. Calhoun of South Carolina, and they were led by Henry Clay of Kentucky, just starting a national political career that would include a record run as Speaker of the House.

This group soon became known as the "War Hawks" for their enthusiastic embrace of hostilities. Residing in areas with no seaports, the War Hawks did not focus on the British maritime maneuvers as motivations for war. But they did have their own grudge against the British. Great Britain continued to have a presence on the North American continent, causing trouble for westward expansionists by inciting Native American tribes. If New England prowar advocates wanted merely to be free of British and French restrictions, the War Hawks' reasons for going to war had a more imperial cast. They wanted to expel British and any other foreign influence from the continent once and for all, leaving no bar to acquiring land in what was then Canada, Florida, and Texas—in fact, all lands to the west, south, and north.

The noisy War Hawks presented James with a particular problem. Had he absolutely no intention of engaging with Great Britain, he could have simply dismissed, denigrated, or ignored them. But if James had to go to war, as increasingly it seemed so, their energy and conviction would help in winning over those reluctant to support war. As always,

James's strategy was to create unity in assembling a common cause, even if that cause was war. As president, James could not come out on one side or the other until he had made his decision, so he and Dolley used her presence as a sort of placeholder, a way of signaling that though James could not officially embrace the War Hawks' agenda, he was not discounting it.

During this time, Dolley and Henry Clay made several noted and publicized appearances. It seems not only was Henry flattered by the attention of the most famous woman in the United States, but he also had a genuine affection for her he would retain for decades. For her part, Dolley could enjoy the charming young man as well as appreciate his potential political use. Stories of their witty sparring made the rounds, such as when Henry declared, "Everybody loves Mrs. Madison," to which Dolley replied, "That's because Mrs. Madison loves everybody."

There seems to have been no hint of sexual impropriety in the stories that circulated, unless one counts the symbol of sharing a snuffbox. Both Dolley and Henry Clay partook of the addicting substance, and Dolley's public sharing of her snuffbox was "read" by all and sundry as a sign of Henry's favor within the Madison administration. Sarah Gales Seaton, like many, thought taking snuff a bad habit but admitted that in Dolley's hands, the snuffbox "seems only a gracious implement with which to charm." Margaret Bayard Smith saw it as "a most magical influence" in soothing savage political breasts. "For who could partake of its contents offered them in a manner so cordial and gracious and retain a feeling inimical to the interests of the bestower[?]" In this way, Dolley kept Henry Clay on a political string, as it were, while James decided what to do.

The official declaration of war on June 18, 1812, delighted the War Hawks, who, upon hearing the news, according to congressional lore, did an "Indian" war dance around their boardinghouse table. It also secured James's reelection in November. It was a close election, and it was the support of the western War Hawks, led by Dolley's "highly valued friend" Henry Clay, that made the difference. But ironically, James's most decisive move only accelerated the divisions, further endangering national unity. Republicans may have celebrated the declaration with parades and cannon fire, but in the Northeast, flags hung at half mast, and church bells tolled mournfully. The Federalists, most of whom were from New England, with their capital tied up in shipping, felt the brunt of war most keenly, and the various Republican groups seized on the situation to make any political hay they could, fostering opposition to the Madison administration.

But objections were not merely for politics' sake; many believed that the declaration came too soon and the United States was not ready for war. The new nation simply did not have the proper military infrastructure, especially in the rudimentary navy. The declaration of war only increased the pressure on James, especially when he learned that two days before the declaration, the British government had repealed the Orders in Council that had restricted neutral trade and was one of the main reasons for going to war.

But it was too late to stop the martial momentum. Anonymous letters and newspaper stories spoke of threats to the president and assassinations by "dagger or poison." Dolley was particularly concerned about stories of spies, disguised as women, coming to the White House to steal James's papers. As the national capital and federal seat, Washington City felt even more unease, as the residents worried it might become a target. Wartime tension made some a bit deranged. A well-known Washington woman drove directly to the White House, stood up in her carriage, let down her long hair ("celebrated for its length"), and declared she would happily cut it in order to hang the president. In a rare break from her public demeanor of good spirits and serenity, Dolley let it be known that "it [would be] difficult to forgive this insult to her husband."

The president was in what moderns would call a public relations nightmare. Though the people of the time did not have the vocabulary, they recognized his dilemma as such. After the declaration, Virginia representative William Burwell worried to his wife, Letitia, that "the difficulties of his situation have increased in a great degree." His only hope lay in "influenc[ing] public sentiment by [some] brilliant achievement."[1] Unfortunately for James, the war went badly right from the beginning, so the Madisons' chance for a "brilliant achievement" lay with Dolley.

Correspondingly, Dolley's wartime efforts intensified. Her "brilliant achievement[s]" were not the dramatic stuff of military victories and battles at sea. Their execution and effects were subtler, if as significant. In the first congressional season after the declaration, Dolley began her "social campaign" early, returning to the capital after only one week at Montpelier, according to her, "in the midst of business & anxiety—anxious for the fate of the War, *only*." Throughout the war, she gave more parties than ever before. These parties reflected the increased need for unofficial space, as people thronged to the capital city. They also reassured the citizens of the District, who kept hearing rumors of invasion, and in the increasingly agitated political atmosphere, they provided a neutral ground for members of the government.

Dolley Madison could be seen as a model for the political wife and would be used as the model for all future First Ladies. She was a superlative example of both because in addition to succeeding at all the practical parts of the job, using the unofficial sphere in its best way and to its full, from the beginning of her husband's term, she also acted as a charismatic figure. Not everyone has this capacity for symbolizing, to convey psychological messages about her husband and his administration, but Dolley did. Now, with America at war, she took that symbolizing capacity to a new level.

During wartime it is crucial to have national unity, and governments will employ a variety of techniques to unite a people during a time of crisis; for instance, appealing to patriotism, inducing fear, calling for collective sacrifice. With a badly divided nation under his watch and a boisterous Congress at his doorstep, James could do little. Because partisan politics were so heated, he could not be seen in any neutral way. But Dolley could.

Though personally she was as partisan as any man in Congress, because she was a woman, she could not hold any official power; under coverture, she could not even own herself. Consequently, Dolley could be seen as politically neutral. Men of parties had "interests" dictated by their political needs, but women could be "disinterested," simply patriotic for their own sakes. Dolley had always personified her husband and his administration. Now her work transcended her political affiliation. Since men were associated with one party or another, no male, not even the president, could represent the United States. Because she was (in theory) above politics, Dolley could appear to the American public and European observers as a larger-than-life embodiment of disinterested patriotism and the nation.

During the War of 1812, Dolley, then, became the charismatic figure not just for James Madison but for the nation's capital. She had always brought people together; now her abilities to draw people in had an urgent, larger purpose. Her mission was to convey to the capital and the country that the government was working and the war was being conducted well. She presented a picture of calm optimism and in her mission was aided by her female colleagues. Both of her sisters, Anna and Lucy, came to Washington for the congressional seasons during the war years to help with the increased need for entertaining. Dolley corralled "a multitude of Beauties" to attract and entertain male visitors. Dolley was only half-joking when she compared her own campaign to a military one: she called up her troops as any general would. In her urging to Sarah Gales Seaton to make her appearance at a "Wednesday night," Dolley implored her "not to desert the standard [flag] altogether."

During the American Revolution, women had organized themselves into spinning bees, producing homespun cloth that allowed the rebelling colonists to wean themselves off imported and unpatriotic British cloth. Embargoes and Non-Importation Acts had not worked in this clash with Great Britain, but Dolley deliberately invoked the spirit of the earlier time by hosting "fringe parties" for the ladies of Washington, who produced not cloth but braided white cotton trim for epaulets worn by the militia.

Society thrived in Washington City during the war years, both the cause and the consequence of Dolley's efforts. Businesses, such as shipping, importing, and others, could not function during the hostilities, and many involved in those industries took a trip to Washington to see their president and how things were going. Locals noted, too, that there were more members' wives in town during the 1812–1813 season than ever before. Wartime Washington was a lively place, and many could not keep up with the crush. Margaret Bayard Smith chided herself for falling down on her calling duties, managing to visit "only" fifty families in one week. Dolley, known for her indefatigable calling, must have easily surpassed that number.

And on Wednesday night, everyone ended up at the drawing room. As always, many commented on the "brilliant scenes," the colorful and stimulating company, further enlivened with men in uniform. Dolley kept up the pace, though the phrase she used at that time, "routine gaiety," indicates the work it took to produce these "brilliant scenes." Before the war, her drawing rooms became known as "squeezes" because of the two to three hundred guests crammed into the Oval Room; wartime Wednesdays regularly housed five hundred. That first month of the congressional season after declaration, Dolley's butler left for France, and she told her cousin and James's personal secretary, Edward Coles: "I am acting in his Dept. & that the city is more *than ever* crouded with strangers!! My head is *dizy*."

The news from the land campaigns was not good. James Madison and his advisors had expected an easy invasion of Canada, given the small population. But they met with surprising resistance from Canadians, who did not want to join the United States. In her personal correspondence, Dolley reflected on developments soberly. When she heard of the "disgraceful conduct" of General Hull, who surrendered to the British at Detroit, she exclaimed to Edward: "Genl. Hull had surrender'd Detroit, *himself* & the whole Army to the British! Do you not tremble with resentment, at this treacheorus act?"

By New Year's 1813, William Burwell reported that "Mr. Madison is in a most perilous situation unless he can impress more energy into the Army than heretofore. . . . Disgust will prevail everywhere." The month that William Burwell made his prediction, James instigated the required personnel changes, and, as often was the case, Dolley was there to soften the blow, keeping the confrontations as calm as possible. As the *New England Palladium* noted, a few days before James asked Secretary of the Navy Paul Hamilton to resign, his wife suspected that bad news was on the way, on account of "the great attention paid her by Mrs. Madison."

The *Palladium* stated confidently that everyone knew that "whenever any of the *great state dependents* are to be sacrificed," James called on Dolley, "who knows everything going on—and indeed moves many things." She focused on the female family members of an endangered man, whom she treated with "more than common attention and civility." In addition to replacing Paul Hamilton with William Jones, James replaced Secretary of War Eustis with John Armstrong.[2]

The public face of Dolley was always supportive and not questioning. Military troops had begun honoring her by parading past her house when she was the wife of the secretary of state. Now, they marched by the White House in order to be reviewed by her, and she did so as a general would. Dolley then invited the soldiers in and served them refreshments, "giving liberally of the best of the house."

She made much of the few military victories that came the United States' way, and the men responsible. In one famous story, she contravened James's order for General William Henry Harrison to return to the battlefield immediately after coming to Washington to report on a successful military action. Dolley wanted him to appear at that evening's drawing room, knowing that not only did the public want to see him and honor him, but they needed to.

The biggest military surprise of the War of 1812 was how well the navy performed. Most assumed that the American victories would be on land, such as the invasion of Canada was supposed to be. After all, as they did in the Revolution, the Americans fought on home turf. Not only was the US Navy woefully underdeveloped, but the British Royal Navy was considered the best in the world. Nevertheless, technical innovations and gifted leadership ensured that the smaller, defter vessels of the American navy won several significant victories. In the 1812 naval campaign, American forces captured the British ships *Guerrière* and *Macedonian*, and officers presented the captured ships' colors, or flags, to Dolley in very public ceremonies.

As the president's secretary, Edward Coles arranged the first of these presentations. In a culture where intelligence traveled slowly, such displays were a welcome source of good news, both informing the public and heartening them. Dolley was conscious of this honor paid to her and the country. During the presentation of the *Macedonian*'s colors, Sarah Gales Seaton noted the flush of pride and patriotism that suffused Dolley's face: "I saw her color come and go."

As always, Dolley's visibility cut both ways, and her position as a "disinterested" patriot did not go unquestioned. Political enemies tried to turn events against her. Federalist Massachusetts congressman Samuel Taggert spread stories of Dolley defiantly stamping on the colors laid before her, thus tarnishing the United States' world reputation: "An Englishman in the city hearing this report basely observed that Charlotte, meaning the Queen of Great Britain, would not have done so with the American colours."

Discussing this incident later in her life, Dolley denied making such a gesture, and, indeed, the story seems unlikely. Such a public display of negativity seems out of character for a woman of such control and consciousness; in addition, that Federalists circulated the story seems suspicious. According to Dolley, when the men had been carrying the flag to her by the corners, "Commodore Stuart let his end fall, either by accident or design (the motive has been much questioned . . .)." According to her, it was another lady cried out, "'trample on it trample on it!'" Dolley drew back saying, "'Oh! not so!,' while the Lady advanced and put her foot on it!"

One of the proofs of the effectiveness of Dolley's efforts lay in the Federalists' reactions and their attempt to use either her self or her unofficial sphere to make their statements. To celebrate the victories at sea, a "splendid dinner" was held, and two hundred people attended, but not one Federalist, though many had been invited. Such churlishness was noted with amusement, and people joked that the French-hating Federalists were "reserving themselves to celebrate the Russian victories over Napoleon," referring to the hostilities between France and Russia.

The first full year of the war ended soberly, the early naval victories overshadowed by the British response to them, which was to blockade the entire eastern seaboard, further strangling business, trade, and the livelihoods of the port cities. From the start of hostilities, what Dolley called the "melancholy business" of war had occupied everyone's thoughts and conversations, being the chief topic of discussion whenever people got together. But in those first days, Washingtonians did not feel the effects of war directly; the actual fighting, on land and sea, took place far from the capital.

By the second year of the war, however, with the British firmly embargoed in the nearby Chesapeake River, local families began to fear that the District might prove an easy and irresistible target. It did not help matters when those in the capital began to hear tales of civilian intimidation wrought by the commander of British naval operations, Sir George Cockburn. Americans considered attacks such as the one on the civilians in nearby Havre de Grace harbor in Maryland "barbaric." The British forces pillaged and destroyed property, but, surprisingly, when the local women pled for their homes, Cockburn, "the Beast of Havre de Grace," relented.

He showed no mercy, however, for another nearby target, Craney Island in Norfolk, Virginia. Not only did the British forces destroy property, but they also raped women. Shocking stories of white women raped not only by soldiers but also by enslaved men and African American freemen only added to Washingtonians' unease. The situation proved fertile ground for rumors, and by the summer of 1812, Dolley was writing to Edward Coles: "If I could, I would describe to you the fears & alarms, that circulate around me. For the last week all the City & G. Toun [nearby Georgetown] (except the Cabinet) have expected a visit from the Enimy, & ware not lacking in their expressions of terror & *reproach*." With her parenthetical reference to the cabinet, Dolley was reflecting the general dynamic of the situation—that locals were as convinced of British invasion as firmly as the government was not.

The "reproach" was directed to the federal and local officials, though Dolley defended James, informing Edward that "we are makeing considerable efforts for defence. The Fort is repairing, & 500 Militia, with perhaps as many regulars are; & *to be*, stationd on the green near the *Wind Mill*, or rather, near Majr. Tayloes." Twenty tents were already up, and they "allready look[ed] well" to Dolley, "as I have allways been an advocate for fighting when *assailed*." Dolley added that "tho a *Quaker*," she kept a Tunisian saber within reach.

Dolley's friends and government officials tried to stay calm. Margaret Bayard Smith confessed to her sister Jane that she had not really ever felt that the United States was at war until that summer, but that "there is so little apprehension of danger in the city, that not a single removal of person or goods has taken place." Virginia congressman William Burwell, still in the capital serving in Congress, also downplayed the rumors to Letitia, his worried wife at home: "I assure you, upon my honor, I do not believe there is the smallest cause for alarm." He took as his proof the behavior of the ladies led by Dolley Madison: "I do not perceive the least alarm among the women; they perceive the ample means taken to defend them and are well aware of their safety."

But the rumors only grew, and signs of panic began to appear. The *National Intelligencer*, always hitherto responsive to a Republican president's situation, began printing atrocity stories that only fanned the flames. Dolley Madison had always stood in for her husband, and her symbolic value was appreciated by friend and foe alike, albeit in different ways. Cockburn fed the rumors of invasion by threatening her. While relating to Edward the details of the plot wherein British "*Rogues*" were to land at Alexandria under cover of darkness and set fire to the White House, Dolley confessed: "I do not tremble at this, but feel *affronted* that the Admiral . . . should send me notis that he would make his bow at my Drawing room *soon*." Surely her bravado was a bit of a pose; Dolley could be forgiven for dreading a man with what she called a "savage stile of warfare."[3]

The summer passed, and the invasion fears died down, but only for a while. The government felt vindicated in its firm stance in the face of civilian panic. As 1813 turned into 1814, the locals dealt with the atmosphere of anxiety by joining in the denial. The reasons that the British would not attack were numerous—the capital was too far from the coast, Baltimore was a more alluring target, and so forth. However, the tide of war was turning, and though it was doing so far from the capital, Washington City would soon feel its effects. In April, Napoleon abdicated, and the end of the war between France and England allowed the British to turn their full attention to the United States, dealing with their former colony once and for all.

They did so by increasing their raids on the East Coast, bottling up the coastline as far north as Maine and as far south as the Gulf Coast. The Chesapeake coastline, with Baltimore and Washington City nearby, was far too tempting a target to ignore. For all the reasons that Washington residents and the government had for thinking Washington not a likely target, the British had two strong reasons for invading the federal seat. First, they could revenge themselves for the looting of York, the British capital in Canada, by American forces. Second, they perfectly understood the immense psychological value of capturing the nation's capital, the president, and his wife.

James had long feared what would happen to the Anglo-American conflict if and when the Napoleonic wars concluded. On July 1, 1814, he called an emergency cabinet meeting to outline his plans. With the regular army far-flung, serving from Canada to New Orleans, he was depending on militia and local forces to hold the capital. He planned to deploy 2,000 to 3,000 armed men between the coast and Washington, with between 10,000 and 12,000 militia on standby in nearby states. Accordingly, James formed the Tenth Military District, with Brigadier General William Winder in charge.

This was not a bad plan, but like so many of James's plans and assumptions about this war, it all came to nothing. Winder continued to believe that invasion would never come, a belief reinforced by the similar attitude of the secretary of war, General John Armstrong. Even after the British landed in Maryland later in July, Armstrong insisted: "No! No! Baltimore is the place, Sir; that is of so much more consequence."

Dolley's mission of reassuring all that the government was in control escalated as the summer passed, and she focused even more on the capital residents. In a letter to her son, Payne Todd, in Paris as part of a peace mission (and mindful that her letters might be leaked), she relayed with bravado: "The British on our shore's are stealing & destroying private property, rarely comeing to battle but when they do, are allways beaten. . . . If the War should last 6 months longer the U. S. will conquer her Enimies."

But these brave words were for public consumption should her letters fall into the wrong hands as they traveled across Europe. Writing to Hannah Nicholson Gallatin in Philadelphia, she expressed her real worries and tensions: "We have been in a state of purturbation here, for a long time—the depredations of the Enemy approaching within 20 miles of the City & the disaffected, makeing incessant difficulties for the Government." Dolley worried about "the disaffected" as much as invading soldiers.

For one who had worked so hard to unify the various populations in the capital, Dolley gave vent to her frustration: "Such a place as this has become I can not discribe it—I wish (for my own part) *we ware* at Phila." But, Dolley added, "the people" would not let them leave, even if they wanted to—"among other exclamations & threats they say if Mr. M. attempts to move from *this House*, in case of an attack, they will *stop him* & that he shall *fall with it*—I am not the least alarmed at these things, but entirely disgusted, & determined to stay with him." Perhaps there was still some bravado in her declaration to Hannah, but it was true that as late as August 6, 1812, Dolley told Hannah, "We are still without an idea of going from hence."

The invasion of Washington City began early in the morning hours of August 19, 1814, as a British force of 4,000 landed at Benedict, Maryland, the main port of the Patuxent River. Couriers brought the news to the capital, including Admiral Cockburn's boast that he intended to dine in Washington in two days. Dolley remained Cockburn's rhetorical focus, as he "sent word to Mrs. Madison that unless she left, the house would be burned over her head."[4] He did not mention James in this boast, nor did Cockburn include the president when he also threatened to parade Dolley through the London streets as a prisoner of war.

It seems too hard to believe that Secretary Jones still believed that Cockburn's warnings were idle threats, but finally, along with Winder, local landowner John Van Ness, and Secretary of State James Monroe, he began to make belated plans for protecting the city. On August 23, James left the White House in order to review the troops in the field, and the *National Intelligencer* reported the rumor that 5,000 or 6,000 British troops had joined the force already in Maryland. Panic broke out in Washington City, beginning a mass exodus. Alone in the White House, except for her servants and slaves, Dolley did what she always did to try to quell the panic. Aware that all eyes were on her, she planned a dinner party.

9

Washington Divided

Dolley's Work for Unity Under Fire

Without question, Dolley's most famous day—August 24, 1814, the day of the invasion of Washington—presents in microcosm all of her work for unity. How she spent the last day of the first White House modeled the purposes for which Dolley had used her creation. The capital city was in crisis, all the divisions that so worried Dolley and James had split, and instead of coming together, Washington City was falling apart. In order to pull the local and official folk together, to send a message of calm and peace, Dolley invited residents and members of the government to a dinner, a meal held in the middle of the day. She intended to do this precisely in the face of the rumors of the invasion; as the rumors strengthened and the city began to evacuate, she continued to prepare for the dinner.

The night before, Dolley began a letter to her sister Lucy, and as the sun rose on the twenty-fourth and Dolley made preparations for her dinner, Dolley wrote to her sister a kind of minute-by-minute account. She also began packing and sending off official papers, including James's notes on the Constitutional Convention. In between packing, dinner preparations, and writing, Dolley ran to the top floor of the president's house with her spyglass, "watching with unwearied anxiety hoping to discern the approach of my dear husband and his friends." James was still out in the field, leaving Dolley in command of the house she had created. Dolley was deciding whether she, too, would have to evacuate.

She had little guidance; on the one hand, the overconfident General Armstrong assured her that there was no danger, and on the other, Dr. James H. Blake, mayor of Washington, made two visits to beg her to flee.

Dolley did not see James all that long day, instead noting with alarm the "military wanderings" of the troops, who seemed to show "a lack of arms or of spirit to fight for their own firesides!" Her reading was correct; that afternoon, in Bladensburg, Maryland, the British would rout the Americans so quickly that they would go "flying t[h]rough the city," earning the battle the derisive title "the Bladensburg races." Her choice was to wait for James to return and make the decision about whether they, too, would evacuate.

Dolley's little sister Anna was still in town as well. That day, Anna sent an anguished note to her sister: "tell me for gods sake where you are and what [you are] going to do. . . . We can hear nothing but what is horrible here—I know not who to send this to—and will say but little." Even at the point of invasion, when Dolley could have worried merely about external enemies, the problem of internal divisions still embittered her. In her letter to Lucy, she intoned bitterly: "Disaffection stalks around us."

It soon became apparent that the dinner party would have to be canceled. Eleanor Jones, the wife of the secretary of war, sent a note as polite as it was understated: "In the present state of alarm and bustle of preparation, for the worst that may happen, I imagine it would be mutually convenient, to dispense with the enjoyment of your hospitality today and therefore pray you to admit this as an excuse for Mr. Jones, Lucy, and myself." William Jones evidently finally believed that the British would attack, as his wife reported that he was sending out the marines, and "Lucy and myself are busy packing."

Dolley's white servant, "French John" Sioussat, "offered to spike the cannon at the gate and lay a train of powder which would blow up the British should they enter the house." Dolley vetoed his plan; she may have feared that such an aggressive act would anger any conquering troops, who might take it out on civilians. Meantime Madison slaves Paul Jennings and Sukey, along with Sioussat, accelerated their evacuation efforts; they did not even bother to clear the dinner table. They rushed around, securing hard-to-find transport and packing and sending the White House silver, cabinet papers, and even the famous red velvet curtains.

Dolley felt keenly the public trust; she knew the White House and all its possessions belonged to the American people, and she felt guilty about possibly having to abandon them. She deliberately sacrificed the Madisons' personal property in order to save what she could of the public's.

One of the objects that Dolley saved ensured her place in history. That it did so ratified her judgment, made at a moment's notice. By the late afternoon of the twenty-fourth, it was becoming increasingly clear that she and her staff needed to leave. Still, she took precious time (and against the urging of some Madison supporters who came to escort her to safely) to direct John Sioussat and Paul Jennings to wrestle the famous Gilbert Stuart painting of George Washington from the wall and out of its frame. She gave it to "two gentlemen of New York," who were passing by, for safekeeping under a "humble but safe roof." In many ways, this act became the defining and lasting image of the War of 1812.

Later in her life, Dolley explained why she took valuable time to secure this portrait as testimony of "my respect for General Washington." Evidence suggests that the portrait that Dolley saved was not even the original Stuart but a copy, and that Dolley knew that. But copy or not did not matter. Dolley knew what it would mean to the American public if this portrait was burned or otherwise destroyed or, even worse, captured as a prize of war and paraded through the London streets, as Admiral Cockburn threatened to do with her. She was correct. Throughout her career as James's political partner, Dolley had shown herself the master of psychological politics, and this was her crowning stroke.

Finally, Dolley's decision was made for her. As Paul Jennings recounts, James Smith, an African American freeman sent by the president from the battlefield, galloped up to the White House, crying, "'Clear out, clear out! General Armstrong has ordered a retreat!'" Dolley crammed the last of the silver in her small drawstring purse, and she and Sukey climbed aboard a carriage containing her sister Anna and Anna's husband, Richard Cutts, driven by an impatient Charles Carroll. As she later told Mary Hazelhurst Latrobe: "I left the house where Mr. Latrobe's elegant taste had been justly admired, and where you and I had so often wandered together." They took off, stopping that day first at Navy Secretary Jones's house and then Carroll's own Belle Vue, and finally spending the night at Matilda Lee Love's Rokeby, across the river in Virginia.

Paul Jennings and John Sioussat were the last to leave. Poignantly, French John locked the front door and then carried Polly, Dolley's beloved macaw, over to the French minister's quarters, the Octagon House. James Madison finally arrived at the White House in the late afternoon. After pausing for refreshment, James set out to catch up with his wife, but not before he ordered John Sioussat to give out brandy to the weary troops. It was *almost* the last party the house would ever see. Paul Jennings hung about the city, curious to see what would happen. He was dismayed to observe that as the shadows of evening fell, the "rabble" came looting the executive mansion, stealing silver and anything else they could carry.[1]

Over the next days, Dolley and James wandered the countryside, missing each other at designated meeting places. The city they had built, the house on which Dolley and Henry Latrobe had lavished so much care and labor, all came to ashes. At sundown on August 24, Vice Admiral Sir George Cockburn and Major General Robert Ross led the British troops into Washington City. They burned the Senate and House of Representatives, including the Library of Congress.

By the time they got to the White House, they were tired and hungry. In a sad parody of Dolley's work, the British soldiers sat down to the last White House dinner party, partaking of the "elegant and substantial repast" set out. The soldiers toasted the king with James's wine. Deprived of his human prize, Cockburn captured her portrait to "keep Dolley safe and exhibit her in London." He also took her seat cushion and, among "pleasantries too vulgar to repeat," remarked that he wished to "warmly recall Mrs. Madison's seat."

After dinner, men ran through the White House rooms setting random fires. But the British had ways of guaranteeing total destruction. The troops broke the windows and tossed in what one witness called "machine[s] of wild-fire," dinner plate–sized spheres that contained hot coals. The machines did their job, beginning "an instantaneous conflagration." Washington residents "stood in awful silence," as "the city was light and the heavens redden'd with the blaze."

As the troops moved next door to burn the Treasury, Captain Thomas Tingey, the American commander of the Navy Yard, ordered the buildings, stores, and ships in the Yard blown up so that the enemy should not have them. The fires set by the British and the explosions set by the Americans frightened the Washingtonians left in the city. Not surprisingly, they felt that the world was coming to an end, including what Anna Maria Brodeau Thornton mourned as "our poor undefended & devoted city." From separate locations in the Virginia countryside, Dolley and James saw the flames in the sky and grieved.

On the second day of the invasion, the British continued to destroy the Departments of War and State, as well as the papers and type of the offices of the *National Intelligencer*, in retaliation for all of the derogatory stories that the editor, Joseph Gales, had written about the admiral. Bent on even more revenge for the editorial assaults, Cockburn intended to burn the building itself but was deterred when he learned that it was not Gales's own property. For all of the viciousness of the attack, the British destroyed little private property and spared civilian lives. They even exempted the Patent Office from destruction after Dr. William Thornton pleaded with them to spare it for the sake of human knowledge.

The ravage of the city might have gone on for days but two incidents put a halt to the British forces. One was a grisly accidental explosion at Greenleaf's Point, about two miles from the Capitol. One hundred and thirty barrels of gunpowder inadvertently exploded, leaving a crater twenty feet deep and forty feet across, killing thirty British soldiers at once, and burying others alive. The second halt to the proceedings came from nature. By early afternoon, hurricane-force winds and rains descended on the city, turning the sky alternatively black as night with "heaving black clouds of rain," and then as bright as day with fierce lightning shows. Americans saw this display as a gift from Providence, as the rain put out the fires; the British saw it as a manifestation of God's wrath at their pillage.

Whatever the intentions of God or nature, the two incidents had the effect of quashing the British taste for revenge. Cockburn led the troops out of the city that night, and the British continued their march to Benedict, Maryland, taking nearby Fort Warburton and Alexandria, Virginia. By mid-September, they were trying to take Baltimore, the location most had believed would be the real prize for British invaders. During the heavy fighting, when British forces unsuccessfully tried to take Fort McHenry, Frances Scott Key, inspired by the sight of the flag flying over the fort, composed a poem, "The Star-Spangled Banner," which he set to the tune of an old drinking song. The song caught on, as renewed war fever took over America. Over the next few months, the British left the mid-Atlantic, heading for the troublesome US troops in the Gulf of Mexico.

When Dolley and James returned to Washington City four days after they had fled, they found their capital city in ruins. The whole city was in chaos, but of course it was the sight of the White House that most emotionally affected the pair. Nothing was left of the executive mansion but its "cracked and blackened walls." The words that people used to describe the fallen house stressed the fragility and vulnerability not just of the symbol of the republic, but of the republic itself—"unroofed," "naked," "cracked," and "defaced." Lawyer William Wirt tried to describe to his wife what he saw during a walk through the ruins, but "I cannot tell you what I felt as I walked amongst them." Dolley could never speak of the sight without emotion, and at the moment, spying passing American soldiers, Dolley wished that "we had ten thousand such men as were passing *to sink our enemy to the bottomless pit.*"

When William Wirt called on James, he found the president "miserably shattered and woebegone . . . heart-broken." In James's mind what had happened was less an invasion by a recognized enemy than a culmination of betrayal and lack of unity. He felt let down by commanders who were either duplicitous or incompetent or both and by his fellow Americans. Instead of focusing on the British troops, James's mind was "full of the New England sedition," to the point at which William tried to change the subject. Still James continued to "press it—painful as it obviously was to him . . . his heart and mind were painfully full of the subject."

Margaret Bayard Smith found Dolley equally inconsolable, "much depressed, she could scarcely speak without tears." Dolley confessed to her friend and colleague Mary Hazelhurst Latrobe that she was so angry she wished she had stayed and fired on the troops: "I confess that I was so unfeminine as to be free of fear, and willing to remain in the Castle!" She did not spare her countrymen from blame, even as she lamented: "If I could have had a cannon through every window; but alas! those who should have placed them there fled before me, and my whole heart mourned for my country!"

Dolley and James were not alone in seeing something beyond mere incompetence or refusal to see reality in the military neglect of the capital city. This was a political culture attuned to discern cabal and plot in any instance, and there was much grist for the rumor mill. The "public voice" accused General Armstrong of wanting the federal seat destroyed so that it could be moved to another location.

In the face of this disaster, unity was no mere abstract concept. In early republican Washington, bringing people together under a banner of civility and common purpose was never just about being nice; it was a matter of survival. Dolley and James turned their attention to the capital, as the burning of Washington City had a paradoxically unifying effect on the nation at large.

The British had gambled on their actions demoralizing the American troops, but of course, such a dramatic gesture could have the opposite effect. The appalling act mobilized American outrage and, except for a small pocket of dissent in the heart of Federalist country, vanquished opposition to "Mr. Madison's war." Politicians who opposed the war, such as DeWitt Clinton, agreed that the question was no longer "whether the war was just or unjust in its commencement." The only question was whether Americans would now fight for their country, and the answer seemed to be a resounding "Yes!"[2] The burning of Washington may have been a lost battle, but it won the war of public support for which the Madisons had been working.

The theory about General Armstrong's motive, whether or not true in his case, reflected a larger truth. The location of the federal seat on the Potomac had been contested from the start. It had been the product of a compromise, and from the first arrivals, there had been complaints about the heat, the roads, the lack of amenities and society. Ironically, the negative feelings about the early capital were so pervasive that the inferiority complex they engendered might have contributed to the notion that Washington City was not an important enough target and that, as Armstrong had asserted, "Baltimore is the place . . . of so much more consequence."

As early as August 27, Philadelphia was offering to house the federal government, and many voices clamored for a relocation to Philadelphia, New York, Baltimore, or one of a dozen other places. Some saw the move as a temporary retrenchment; others had always assumed that the capital city would never stay in Washington. The invasion just hastened the inevitable.

Such a move would have been disastrous for several reasons. Most immediately, it would have bankrupted the local families who had invested in the capital city. A decision to move, according to Margaret Bayard Smith, would "in one night, have hundreds of our citizens been reduced from affluence to poverty." Of course, the government had no obligation to these citizens, as some congressmen would eventually argue, as the good of the government should be the primary concern.

But it would have also taken months to make such a move, delaying the government's recovery. Americans were also beginning to discern the power of the psychological in politics: What would it mean for the American government to be seen, in essence, in retreat? As the *Daily Intelligencer* framed the issue: "It would be kissing the rod an enemy had wielded: it would be deserting the seat of government at the dictation of any enemy!"

James called Congress back early to decide the issue, and on September 19, they gathered in Blodgett's Hotel to debate the question of relocation. Expected to last several days, the discussions took four and a half months. The first vote tested the waters, to see if the government should even consider relocating, and that vote was grim. Seventy-nine voted for opening the debate, mostly Northern states, with thirty-seven, from Pennsylvania and the Southern states, voting to keep the capital.

During the debates, Dolley once again did what James could not. She allied herself with the locals, families with whom she had worked and socialized. The first thing the Madisons needed was a base of operations. No matter that John Tayloe, owner of the Octagon House, the finest private residence in the District, was a political opponent of James. He was one of Dolley's friends and gladly gave the presidential couple his home as their temporary White House. Just as local gentry, not the government, had paid for the defense of the city before the invasion, the local banks, not the federal government, made funds available for rebuilding. Leading local men and pro-government officials who had met under Dolley's roof now worked together, raising money to build the "Brick Capitol" in which to house Congress.

The locals showed their loyalty and commitment in many ways. Just a few months after the burning, the Van Nesses built one of the finest private homes in America, a mansion that combined architectural features of an Italian villa and a Southern plantation. Henry Latrobe designed the showplace. Wealthy real estate investor Thomas Law made his contribution artistically as well as financially. He composed poem after poem inspired by "the scenes of conflagration" and then by the rebuilding efforts. Perhaps reflecting the reality of the situation, he deliberately invoked women and female metaphors for the renewal process; his descriptions of the characters of "Columbia," "Liberty," and "Justice" bear striking resemblances to Dolley. A broadside that celebrated "Peace on Honorable terms" depicted "Liberty" and "stern Justice" in buxom, Dolley-like ways.

The ladies of Washington also had their own plan, one that demonstrated their commitment to a city that was staying. Poverty had been a problem in Washington City from the beginning. Laborers poured into the city, ready to work in a building boom that never materialized. The devastation of the city and exigencies of war just made it worse. Dolley and her cohorts had always involved themselves in charity, through visits to the poor and "the cause of general literature [literacy]." Now Dolley teamed up with Margaret Bayard Smith and local heiress Marcia Burnes Van Ness to found the Washington Female Orphan Asylum. The Asylum did not actually open its doors until the next year, but the intention, as well as the actual execution of this project, played its part in healing the city. Dolley became the "First Directress," contributing twenty dollars and a cow; she also made clothes for the orphan girls. Marcia ran the day-to-day operations, and Margaret raised money, auctioning off copies of her books.

Washington City recognized the value of the women's efforts with publicity in the *National Intelligencer*. In this era, women's names, let alone their activities, rarely made the papers, but the *Intelligencer* not only announced the initial planning meeting but also reported on the fundraising efforts and opening ceremonies, calling the new institution "the glory of Washington City" and noting that "a nobler object cannot engage the sympathy of our females."[3]

In the debates raging in Congress, many saw in the calls to remove the federal seat the corruption of "personal motivations"; that is, men who favored removal were suspected of doing so for the favor and reward they might garner by bringing such a prize home to their constituents. While there was certainly an element of personal interest in the anti-Washington position, what is less apparent is that there might be motivations, aside from local investments, guiding those who wanted to stay. For all those who were ready to quit the city, more appreciated the capital community and concomitant opportunities she had created. For fifteen years, she had worked to develop the capital into a real city and a seat of power. Her unofficial sphere had constructed networks of power that implemented political action. For those who had learned to work within them, these structures would be invaluable. Could they be reconstructed in a new location? This seemed doubtful.

Washington City was a unique setting. The very undeveloped nature of the city, with no industry, little society outside of government, no long-standing elites or cultural institutions, meant that it could be a city devoted entirely to politics. A more established city, such as New York or Philadelphia, might offer more amenities, but the presence of a local elite, along with more established social and economic as well as political hierarchies, might interfere with what federal politicians needed to conduct the government business.

The fruits of Dolley's quest for unity manifested itself during this time. The existing historical record does not show conversations directly addressing the issue that Dolley might have had, though no doubt they took place. Still, the cumulative effect of her work spoke for her. Under her hand, the capital city and the White House had become symbols for the nation, and she had succeeded so well that when both came under attack, Americans felt it personally. In the same way, she could not have foreseen that the social and political communities she built would be needed to ensure the federal seat's survival, but they did. How Americans and officials felt about their government—the intangible psychological effect—was a product of Dolley's efforts.

In any event, on October 17, 1814, the resolution for the capital to stay in Washington passed in the House. Dolley's unofficial sphere had been bipartisan, and what carried the day were the Federalists who voted with the Democratic-Republicans. Nine of them voted this way, and the bill passed by nine votes. It would take some more time for the Senate to confirm the House vote, but they did on February 4, 1815, and rebuilding began. Historical hindsight would prove them correct. The country needed a stable capital in order to cement the Union and begin to grow into a full-fledged nation-state.

Ensconced in the Octagon House, Dolley launched the 1814 congressional season only two days after Congress had returned to debate relocation. She gave parties and gatherings, a tangible reminder to those who debated the advantages of the capital's present location. Dolley mourned the loss of her "piano, book cases and other handsome furniture . . . presentation gifts . . . busts and cases of medals." Confessing that she was "nearly *bereft* of furniture & cloaths" she bought pieces of both wherever she could, from the American legation in France and from the Gallatins, who were moving to France. Dolley may have lost her silver, mirrors, and lamps, but she supplied the drama of light for one party by stationing enslaved men throughout the house with pine torches.

What she lacked in props for her political performances she tried to make up for in her person. Some of the descriptions of her most extravagant outfits date from this time. And of course, Dolley still possessed the chief attraction: herself. By August 1815, the Madisons had given John Tayloe his house back and moved into more temporary digs, a set of rooms in the Seven Buildings, at the corner of Pennsylvania Avenue and Nineteenth Street. Mary Boardman Crowninshield visited Dolley in her new setting and mourned the loss of the gorgeous White House furniture, the red velvet curtains replaced by stamped cambric, and the satin-covered sofas with "two little couches covered with blue patch, [and] a small sideboard with I don't recollect what on it." Still, Dolley was Dolley, and Mary added: "You could not but feel at your ease in her company."

Dolley's social strategies had always worked. Her first drawing room in those dark days enjoyed a record attendance, and her popularity, and consequently that of the Madison administration, soared. With the city established, and the example of her success, more families followed in Dolley's wake. In her private letters to family and friends, Dolley confessed to being overwhelmed by "company." In 1816, she reported, "one hundred young ladies in the city—not 10 of them belong to the place."

Always attentive to the mood of her adopted city, Margaret Bayard Smith noted that "the parties became so frequent that our social intercourse degenerated into downright dissipation." But of course, Dolley always had her detractors. The *Washington City Gazette* was disappointed, hoping that the destruction of the White House had "put an end to drawing-rooms and levees; the resort of the idle, and the encouragers of spies and traitors." But the drawing rooms had to continue. They were too important.

Meanwhile, the War of 1812 dragged on. Finally, on December 24, 1814, the American peace commission, made up of Albert Gallatin, John Quincy Adams, Henry Clay, Jonathan Russell, and James Bayard, signed the peace treaty in Ghent. On February 13, 1815, news traveled to Washington City that the Treaty of Ghent had arrived in New York, and by the next day, Henry Carroll, a secretary to the peace commission, arrived in the late afternoon with the document. The terms of peace could have only been disappointing. As regarding territory and boundary issues, the two nations were exactly in the same place as before. The English did not even promise to end impressment—that crucial issue of "national honor." Luckily for the Americans, the practice was already on the wane. The cessation of the Napoleonic wars reduced the need for sailors. And finally, of course, the demand that the Orders in Council be repealed was moot, as they had been so shortly before the declaration of war.

While James and his cabinet were upstairs looking over a document that only conceded what had been conceded before, Dolley was gathering a party downstairs. By early evening, everyone was at Dolley's most portentous drawing room, and according to one reporter, "what a happy scene it was!" Political enemies, who had been "against one another in continual conflict and fierce debate," now moved through the room with "elated spirits" and "softened hearts," cordially felicitating one another. As always, "doing the honors of the occasion" and presiding "with a grace all her own" was Dolley.

The reporter for the *Intelligencer*, Dolley's colleague Margaret Bayard Smith, while describing her as a "queenly beauty" and "in the meridian of life," stressed that "*she* was, in her person for the moment, the representative of the feelings of him who was, at this moment, in grave consultation with his official advisers." No matter what the substance of the document, Washingtonians went "crazy with joy," according to Paul Jennings, at the prospect of war's end.

Dolley's cousin Sally Coles waited outside the door upstairs and, when she got the word, ran to the head of the stairs, calling down to the expectant crowd, "Peace! peace!" The butler, John Freeman, passed out wine to all, and Paul Jennings played "The President's March" on the violin. The association with society and politics was so intertwined that one newspaper illustrated the coming of peace as an event at which "social hearts and cheerful glee / Warm the rapt bosoms of the free."

Dolley's function, as it had been on many occasions, was to reassure: "No one could doubt, who beheld the radiance of joy which lighted up her countenance and diffused its beans around, that all uncertainty was at an end." Margaret Bayard Smith made the pronouncement that "the government of the country had in very truth . . . 'passed from gloom to glory.'"[4] Though in the end the United States gained little from the conflict, Dolley's abilities to unify made even the useless War of 1812 seem like a victory.

10

"A More Perfect Union"
The Madison Legacy

THE MADISONS NEVER lived in the White House again. They finished their second administration in the Seven Buildings, and in the golden glow of approbation that has long puzzled historians. But as the couple boarded the steamboat to a well-deserved retirement, they had achieved a victory of sorts, one that was partial and contested but nonetheless a victory. The Madison administration had none of the "brilliant achievements" that mark a successful presidency. James did not win a great war for the United States or acquire vast territories; the War of 1812 was more of a draw. But his contemporaries recognized that his steadfast adherence to the constitutional principles of a weak executive and guardianship of the people's power preserved the highest ideals of the republic.

Though they did not have the word for it, the citizenry also appreciated the Madisons' use of psychological politics. In the face of a war that won little and cost much, the new Americans had a sense of national unity that they had not had before. Without question, by the way they ruled and reacted during a time of crisis, the couple established and secured Washington City as the national capital. James remained committed to the ideas and ideals of the Revolution, while Dolley worked to make the Revolution real, anchoring James's ideas in practical reality. James and Dolley did not enjoy an unblemished or total success in their policies, but if they were not perfect, they left, in the words of James's major legacy, the Constitution, "a more perfect Union."

One of the reasons it is hard to appreciate and situate the Madisons' work toward unity is because as they left office, their world was undergoing a radical change. Though Dolley was somewhat younger than James, both were essentially eighteenth-century leaders in a world that was rapidly becoming modern. Historians have dubbed the first years of the James Monroe administration that followed the Madisons' as the Era of Good Feelings, but the good feelings of unity and national pride were Madisonian afterglow. James Monroe and his successors over the 1820s and beyond presided over political and cultural changes that utterly transformed the worlds James and Dolley struggled to unite.

Certainly one of the Madisons' goals had been to unite the Republican Party and to finally banish the Federalist "faction." At first glance, it seems they did so, at least in 1817. Following the example of George Washington, Republican James Monroe set out for a months-long goodwill tour across the country, traveling to the Detroit frontier, the farthest west a president had ever been. As the truest proof of the Republican victory, when President Monroe visited Boston, Massachusetts, the heart of Federalism, crowds cheered, and newspapers celebrated.

But that Madison political victory was beside the point, as the political landscape rapidly underwent a massive transformation, and the first institutionalized and recognized party machines emerged to become the hallmark of the US system. Likewise, James and Dolley preserved republican virtues for a nation that would move beyond republicanism to create one of the most effective democracies in the world. Finally, what did James's careful stewardship of presidential power mean when almost every president after him, especially wartime presidents, would extend the power of the presidency?

The world of the nineteenth century would see even more profound changes. As the United States moved toward a cash-based capitalist economy, wild fluctuations and economic upheavals occurred as financial infrastructures adjusted to changing monetary practices, resulting in financial panics in 1819 and 1837. The institution of slavery, which the founders had hoped would just fade away, became more entrenched in the South, as cotton became king, and Northerners came to see it as more of a problem than ever, increasing sectional divides. Slavery became the crux of almost all political clashes on the federal level. Whether it was an argument about a tariff or a public roads project, slavery was often at the heart of the issue. When it was overtly the topic of discussion, such as in the question of how to admit states into the Union, slavery threatened to destroy the United States. The Missouri Compromise of 1820 was one such moment, when the heated rhetoric on both sides threatened to engulf the nation.

Enslaved people themselves took action, and the era saw full-scale slave rebellions, with Denmark Vesey's South Carolina–based conspiracy in 1822 and Nat Turner's Virginia uprising in 1831. Native Americans, too, continued to push back against the new "manifest destiny," as the Monroe Doctrine sanctioned unfettered geographical expansion undreamed of in the days of Washington and Madison.

The 1820s and 1830s also saw threats to the social order as various "others"—women of all races and classes, enslaved and free African Americans, whites from the lower classes—made demands of the United States, based on revolutionary arguments about rights and liberties. In his famous observation of America, Alexis de Tocqueville coined the term "individualism," and the evolution of this American characteristic led to a more market-oriented, self-enrichment ethos, far from James's ideas of subsuming and balancing various interests for the public good. New ideas of religion, of art, of culture pushed long-held beliefs out of the way in the quest for modernity. No wonder that the founders who lived to see the 1820s were shocked at what they had wrought.

With all of this change surging around them, the Madisons remained relatively isolated in their rural retreat, Montpelier. Through the 1820s and 1830s, the world came to them, but it was a particular slice of society. Hordes of admirers, colleagues from the old days, and sightseers came to pay homage to the former president. Occasionally, the world came to James with a request for guidance, and on those occasions it became clear that his concern was always unity.

In 1819, the Missouri Territory applied for admission to the Union as a slave state. New York congressman James Tallmadge started the controversy by proposing to amend their application to prohibit the further introduction of slaves to Missouri and to gradually free the prospective children of slaves already there. As was always the case whenever the topic of slavery arose, the resulting tumult was about more than the issue at hand. The Missouri question brought up the big concerns; to wit, did the Constitution confer on Congress the power to decide issues of slavery?

If Congress had the power to attach an admissions requirement for new states, as Southerners feared, would they eventually abolish slavery? When editor Robert Walsh Jr. asked James Madison to clear up the constitutional issues, he got an answer that was Madisonian in its precision. When Walsh asked if the framers had anticipated this problem of admission of new states and slavery, James answered that their concern at the time lay only in the importation of slaves into the United States: "A power to emancipate slaves was disclaimed; nor is anything recollected that denoted a view to control the distribution of those within the country."

In saying this, James allied himself against those, including his old colleague John Jay, who said the slave trade clause that prohibited the "importation" of slaves also included migration within US borders. James was very clear in his recollection that there was no such understanding among the framers. Indeed, this new interpretation astonished him. Had the Southern delegates at the time even suspected such an elasticity to the clause, there would have been no Constitution.

No doubt James was right, as he usually was when it came to such particulars. Perhaps those who argued that "importation" and "migration" were synonymous were acting disingenuously, attempting to find a loophole that would allow an eventual constitutional prohibition on slavery. It was not as if James came out and defended slavery, as some others did; he was only acting as the recollector of original intentions. Still, this was an occasion for him to have gone further and made a more positive stand against the institution that would one day threaten his beloved Union.

He felt the best way to preserve the Union was to quell the dissent that was at present fueling the Missouri debates. It seems that the nation agreed; they could not settle the question of congressional power once and for all, so they settled on a compromise. Missouri was admitted as a slave state, while Maine was admitted as a free state, keeping the balance even between slave and free states. Further, slavery's expansion was somewhat prohibited by restricting slavery to below the parallel 36/30 North.

Of course, as slavery was one of the major topics of the day, people came to James as both a founder and a Southerner to solve this thorny dilemma. He rarely satisfied them. His was the generation that thought of slavery as a "necessary evil." For these founders, the objections to slavery were not moral but political. That is, James, like many other men of his day, did not object to slavery because it was an unjust institution that treated humans like property. Rather, they worried about the effect of such a depraved institution on white people who would abuse their power over slaves and on the nation at large. They saw themselves as in danger, as well, from slave insurrections. From the start of the republic, before the Declaration was signed, slavery had threatened to split the Union, and that menace continued, shaping everything else that followed, including the formation and ratification of the Constitution.

Like Thomas Jefferson, James could not envision a multiracial society. For the sake of social harmony and political adhesiveness, he thought that the best solution would be to remove the source of threatened strife—the African Americans themselves. In 1816, along with others, James became a founding member of the American Colonization Society (ACS), which aimed to send black people, beginning with the free population, "back" to Africa. The ACS planned that slaves would be bought from slaveholders (thus acknowledging the masters' property rights) with a mix of government and private funds. The ACS got as far as establishing Liberia, on the west coast of Africa, as a place for American blacks to settle. ACS members included both abolitionists and Southern slaveholders who wanted to secure the institution of slavery by ridding the United States of troublesome free blacks.

This scheme was a perfect illustration of one of James's intellectual weaknesses. For him, even though he lived intimately with slaves, African Americans were an abstraction that could be solved like any intellectual puzzle. He did not see that his own slaves had family connections in the United States as deep and meaningful as that of any First Family of Virginia. Nor could he apprehend that free black people, the especial target of the ACS, were as truly American and at home as he was.

Harriet Martineau, the famed English economist and social philosopher, came to visit Montpelier in March 1835. Harriet was one of the formidable intellects of her time, and her remarks about the Madisons showed the same incisiveness she used in all of her observations of America. Harriet was impressed with Dolley's "discretion, partiality, and kindliness," characterizing her as "a strong minded woman, fully capable of entering into her husband's occupations and cares; and there is little doubt that he owed much to her intellectual companionship, as well as to her ability in sustaining the outward dignity of his office."

Harriet also appreciated James as a source of knowledge and information on a variety of topics. But Harriet was a social radical and an abolitionist and was most interested in his thoughts on slavery. James did not so much avoid her questions as he seemed to float above them. Harriet noted that "he talked more on the subject of slavery than on any other" and that "he found himself to be almost in despair." He could not think his way out of it and so found himself clinging to improbable solutions, such as wholesale removal of entire populations as espoused by the ACS.

Harriet was baffled: "How such a mind as his could derive any alleviation to its anxiety from that source is surprising." She attributed this lapse in James's intellectual integrity to his "inexhaustible faith" in the "well-founded commonwealth" to work it out. James just could not see a Union that included everybody, so any person or group who stood in the way of that goal had to go.[1]

As for Dolley, whatever thoughts she had when she reentered a slave society upon her marriage, she seems to have developed a typical slaveholder's perspective, seeing slaves not as full people but as childlike, in constant need of supervision lest they shirk their duties or steal. We have no reflections on what she thought of slavery as a system; rather, the only reactions on record are about particular slaves. Dolley exhibited that curious mixture of familiarity and distance common to people of her culture. For instance, Dolley shared her life with her lady's maid, Sukey. On one hand, Dolley seemed to really care for the woman she described as her "most efficient House servant." In 1833, she even worried about her health in a letter to her family, describing Sukey as "very ill with bilious fever."

On the other hand, in a long, exasperated passage in a letter to her sister, Dolley complained how Sukey stole so much from her that Dolley sent her away for a while. Still, she told Anna, she found "it terribly inconvenient to do without her, & suppose I shall take her again, as I feel too old to undertake to bring up another—so I must even let her steal from me, to keep from labour myself. . . . I would buy a maid but good ones are rare & as high as 8 & 900$—I should like to know what you gave for yours."

In other words, Dolley felt victimized by a woman she could not do without. She could not understand why a person whose labor is in effect stolen every day might steal from her mistress. It is hard to reconcile the cold, hard language of cash that Dolley used in discussing human beings with the woman celebrated by whites for her empathy and warmth. Indeed, though Dolley's attitudes were typical of women of the slaveholding class, put against her public persona, they seem doubly discordant.

While James worried about the nation, Dolley, as she tended to do, kept her eye on the capital. She did not go to Washington during James's retirement, but her many correspondents kept her in touch with "her" city. Dolley was especially concerned with political party discord and its effects on the social life she thought so crucial to the smooth running of government. Like many of the earlier generation, Dolley was fascinated and shocked by the emergence of political parties, as she said while soliciting news from her niece: "I confess I do not admire the contention of parties, political or civil, tho' in my quiet retreat I am anxious to know all the manoeuverings of both, the one and the other, so, be not timid in laying their claims before me, no one shall see statements but myself."

In 1829, a scandal broke in Washington that would have benefited from the intervention of a Dolley Madison. Unfortunately, she was not there, but her correspondents kept her abreast of each development. The Eaton Affair centered around the wife of President Andrew Jackson's secretary of war, John Eaton. With President Jackson a widower, Margaret O'Neale Timberlake Eaton had become the leading lady of the administration. Margaret was a local Washington girl of dubious reputation. It was whispered that, in addition to a general sexual laxity, she had had an affair with John Eaton during her first marriage and before their own.

Both official and local ladies objected to such a woman being placed at the head of society, so they would be forced to interact with her and have her in their homes. Though the ladies were clear on this point, it may be that the reaction to the woman they called Peggy (a derivation of Margaret but one that suggested low-class origins) reflected subconscious fears of the democracy ushered in by Jackson. They tied the ascension of this "common" (in the sense of "vulgar") woman with the emergence of the "common man."

Washington society soon divided into pro-Margaret camps, who would socialize with President Jackson's favorite, and anti-Margaret camps, who snubbed her whenever possible. Dolley, who had always used social events to dial down the temperature of political posturing, was horrified that both factions used parties, balls, and calling practices to make either declarations or protests in the matter. Not surprisingly, male politicians and their families tried to use the Eaton Affair for their various political purposes, thus multiplying and extending its effects.

Dolley mourned, even as she predicted: "The conduct of the P[resident]. & his Cabinet, is indeed astonishing, & exhibits a melancholy perspective, as well as re-trospect to our country—but I doubt not of—*impeachments*, by & by, if they go on in this *lawless*, & unfeeling manner." Dolley was right about the prospect of "impeachments"; with social circles at a standstill, political business could not go on. Eventually, the scandal culminated with the dissolution of the whole cabinet by resignation and dismissal. Such an event had never happened before (or since); the country was thrown off guard and dismayed. Newspapers deemed Margaret Eaton "the Doom of the Republic."

Dolley found all of this distressing. Like many political women, in her writing Dolley denied any interest or facility for politics, even as she asserted her opinions. Dolley had always felt an affinity for diplomats, a feeling they reciprocated. During this time, she wrote to an American diplomat: "In politicks you know, I was never an Adept—I therefore will only observe, that our Country seems now to be entirely of Mr. Laws [Thomas Law, the wealthy Washington developer] opinion that 'Agitation and excitement are happiness.'" She continued: "I hope some, of the Scenes got up in the House of Representatives, *never* reach you as in that case, they would exite even more regret among the considerate here, than they now do."

Dolley and James also had their political protégés. Both continued to be political forces and had much help and guidance to offer the younger generation. Moreover, as the 1820s and 1830s went on, the couple increasingly became valued as symbols of an earlier, purer era. One of the new couples that sought the Madisons' imprimatur was William Cabell Rives and Judith Walker Rives. William was a well-born but not wealthy young man who secured his fortune and his rising political career by marrying the rich and well-connected Judith Walker. Such was the Walkers' place in society that when a government appointment left a seat in Congress vacant, the powerful men of the district "invited" the newest addition to the Walker clan, William Cabell Rives, to assume it.

On their way to Washington, the young couple stopped to pay homage and allegiance to the Madisons. As James imparted his political wisdom to William, as well as letters of introduction to important personages, Dolley drew Judith aside. As Judith recalled in her memoirs, Dolley gave her "a necklace of great beauty" and a diamond cross. "'I have a special fancy,' she said 'that you should wear these during your campaign in Washington. If my friends there should happen to recognize them, they will be as sure a passport to their hearts as the letters of introduction I have given you.'" Judith hesitated to accept such costly gifts, but Dolley insisted, and "the compact was sealed with a warm embrace."[2] Dolley saw this young woman embarked on a political career of her own and, notwithstanding the official letters of introduction, knew that display of her jewelry would "vouch" for Judith where it counted—in people's hearts.

Though people came to James as a source of wisdom, the source of original intentions, the Madisons saw themselves much more as guardians of the past rather then active agents of the future. In their retirements, both Dolley and James took on various projects in order to shape their historical legacy. By far the most absorbing of these projects was one that James also hoped would contribute to his country's sense of its own history, or "veneration," as he called it, and help to hold the republic together. The revolutionary generation was a remarkably self-conscious one, and men such as John Adams and Thomas Jefferson spent a great deal of time and ink positioning themselves in the Pantheon of History, jealously guarding and claiming their legacies.

James, on the other hand, in this as in all matters, was less egotistical; his focus was on the need to preserve and disseminate the history of the nation. From the many accounts by travelers and visitors, it is clear that James loved to talk almost compulsively about the past and issues that faced the founders. He also shared his papers and his thoughts with biographers and anyone interested in writing about the past.

James understood the role of writing in uniting a people, providing them with a sense of shared history and common cause. A sense of "antiquity," as he called it, provided stability to a nation and inspired attachment and loyalty. One of the reasons he waited to publish his own papers was because he wanted enough time to pass that the public would see, for instance, his notes from the Constitutional Convention as documents bathed in the glow of "antiquity."

A great deal of his retirement was spent readying his papers for publication, so much so that it became a family enterprise. He began in earnest during the debates over the admission of Missouri as a slave state, as he realized that the future held many threats to union and he wanted to leave this earth with the record, as he saw it, straight. Dolley, always ready to take on James's projects as her own, joined in, assembling, transcribing, filing, and editing. This was an age before professional archivists of any sex, so in important ways, Dolley was ahead of her time, as a woman literally making history. She worked from ten in the morning to three in the afternoon, part editor, part secretary, and part collector. Dolley took the lead in scouring the Madisons' networks, ferreting out letters from James to a variety of people, included their enemy, John Randolph. Dolley's brother, who lived locally, was also enlisted to aid the grand project.

This was an enormous undertaking, and it contributed to the dynamic of the couple's retirement, in that they tended to stay at home, and the papers project gave them a good reason to do so. As early as 1820, Dolley told her cousin that the project "fixed" them at Montpelier: "This is the third winter in which he has been engaged in the arrangement of papers, and the [business] appears to accumulate as he proceeds—so that I calculate its out-lasting my patience and yet cannot press him to forsake a duty so important, or find it in my heart to leave him during its fulfillment." The work reached its peak in 1823, and by then Dolley's dedication was so professional that she would not even let a bad cold stop her productivity. If illness meant that she could not write, she could at least copy.

Interestingly, when there were editorial decisions to be made, Dolley and James made them in the cause of conciliation and unity. Dolley may have considered James's words to be "sacred and no more to be infringed or altered than his last will," but she also confessed that she did take liberties. Couching them as "consonant to his wishes and direction," but also as with her "concurrence," if she encountered "any letter—line—or word" that "struck me as being calculated to injure the feelings of any one or wrong in themselves that I would withdraw them or it." Historical accuracy, then, could be trumped by hurt feelings. Dolley was James's partner in this project to the end. His final document, "Advice to My Country," was written in her hand.

James intended these papers to be published after his death, precisely for the reasons of history but also as a source of income for his widow. By the late 1820s, it was clear that James, much older than Dolley, was slowing down. James left life as he lived it, modestly and with little fuss. In June 1836, as he lay dying, his physician offered to prolong his life with stimulants so that he, like his predecessors, John Adams and Thomas Jefferson, could die on July 4. With characteristic eschewal for dramatic show, James refused, preferring to die "in the full possession of all his noble faculties," and did so, on June 28, 1836. His faithful slave Paul Jennings was at his side. When he could not eat his breakfast that morning, his niece Nelly Conway Madison Willis asked him, "'What is the matter, Uncle James?'" "'Nothing more than a change of mind, my dear.'" As Paul remembered it: "His head instantly dropped, and he ceased breathing as quietly as the snuff of a candle goes out." He was eighty-five, and Dolley was sixty-eight. They had been married nearly forty-two years.

Dolley, his faithful companion and nurse, almost broke with grief over his death. One thing that kept her going was her determination that his words would live. In her letters written days after his death, she invariably mentioned her devotion to the papers—"Especially do I value all his writings"—along with her own loss. In a reply to a formal letter of condolence from President Andrew Jackson, she declared: "I am now preparing to execute the trust his confidence reposed in me—that of placing before Congress and the World, what his pen had prepared for their use, and with the importance of his Legacy, I am deeply impressed." So much did Dolley see her mission as one of public trust that she published her reply to the president as well as the portions of James's will that pertained to his papers.

To modern Americans, the publication of such an important set of papers seems obvious, and indeed, in the present day, American tax dollars go to supporting various presidential papers projects. But the worth of such a project was not clear to the people of the nineteenth century, and with partisan bitterness still simmering, it was risky to propose that the government sponsor what might be seen as a blatant public relations boon for the Republican Party. Accordingly, Dolley approached private presses first with various schemes, but the process was soon hopelessly bogged down.

The problems were many—for instance, based on a publication of George Washington's papers, James figured that his would be worth $100,000. No press offered anything near that sum, but it was hard for Dolley to move past that number. Complicating things, Dolley entrusted the nuts and bolts of the process to her unreliable and dissolute son, Payne Todd, whom all agreed was "the last man in the world to compass such a business."

In the end, Dolley turned to her old friends and colleagues to help pass a bill in Congress, and eventually Congress published the papers. They gave her $30,000 for the documents that made up the first three volumes, which appeared in 1840. In 1848, they gave her $25,000 for the last four, paying Dolley $5,000 in cash and putting $20,000 in a trust that kept it out of Payne's hands.

Without James, Montpelier proved too lonely and isolated for Dolley, and in 1837 she moved to Washington City for part of each year. In 1844, when debt forced her to sell Montpelier, she became a permanent resident of the capital city. And they were glad to have her. A look at her later Washington career shows some of the fruits of her union building. She became for this next generation of ruling Americans a symbol that transcended politics, not a "relict" just of James Madison (widows were known as "relicts" of their husbands) but of the republic. Of course, politicians of both stripes strove to ensure that some of the luster rubbed off on them, and her endorsement, mostly in the form of her presence, was sought from all sides.

Everyone wanted Dolley, and she obliged as many as she could. Dolley attended inaugurations and other White House events. Her political social calendar became so complicated that she bought a congressional directory and used it as a kind of ledger in order to keep track of visiting "debts." Dolley was very poor at this time of her life; some historians speculate that Dolley did not turn down invitations because she needed to socialize in order to eat. What is clear is that she did not have money for clothes, so she recycled and reused clothes from her heyday. Early photographs of her exist, and in all of them, the viewer sees an antique lady in an antique dress of black velvet, with white trimmings and a white satin turban. She sports the long, richly colored shawls so popular in her day.

Though her sartorial choices spoke of necessity before anything else, Dolley had been so long a symbol to the residents of Washington City that her appearance only reinforced her iconic status in the town. She was living history, and she looked it. She entered the emblematic stage of her life after 1844. At that point, she would know all twelve presidents, having taken tea with George Washington, attended the 1845 inauguration of James Polk, and met with Zachary Taylor.

She performed symbolic acts that imparted new enterprises with the imprint of the founding: sending the first private telegraph message, accepting her own seat on the floor of the House of Representatives, receiving a commemorative medal honoring the War of 1812. The committee in charge of raising the Washington monument drafted her, along with two other iconic widows, Eliza Schuyler Hamilton and Louisa Catherine Johnson Adams, to raise money and interest in the project. At the cornerstone laying ceremony in 1848, Dolley was there, giving the large crowds that turned up for the event the notion that the "executive part of the government was still influenced to some extent by the ideals and practices of an earlier day," a seemingly apolitical endorsement of the present administration.

Sometimes Dolley was treated like an attraction herself. The *Boston Cultivator* deemed her "one of [Virginia's] monuments." Matthew Brady, who would later gain fame as the primary photographer of the Civil War, set out to capture the likenesses of the remnants of the founding generation and sought out Dolley. With his eye, the Dolley left for us and posterity looks like an elder stateswoman—a Minerva, the goddess of wisdom, defender of the state and civilized society. She looks the part of an icon: serene, infinitely wise, and not quite of this world.

With characteristic public modesty, Dolley framed all these honors as "token(s) of their remembrance, collectively and individually, of One who has gone before us"—her late husband, James Madison. As always, Dolley's symbolizing capacity had two sides. Even as she was "standing in" for James at public ceremonies and private events, she was also his place-holder in the growing debates about abolition and slavery.

The American abolition movement, led by William Lloyd Garrison and others, came to public notice in the 1830s and 1840s. When James died in 1836, it was widely expected that he, following George Washington's (if not Thomas Jefferson's) example, would free his slaves. It was obvious to all, however, that to do so would have impoverished Dolley, but that did not stop the wave of disapproval when it was revealed that James left the enslaved people to her and $2,000 to the American Colonization Society.

As Dolley had acted as a lightning rod for James during the fierce partisan debates earlier in the century, at the end of her life she came in for criticism for her continuing slave ownership, and criticism of James also deflected on her. In 1848, Garrison's abolitionist newspaper, the *Liberator*, witheringly wondered at the spectacle of "*the widow of James Madison, the fourth President of the United States*" selling slaves, "not done, let it be noted, in the darkness of the Alabama cotton-field, or of the Louisiana cane-brake, but at the heart of the Federal City—in the midst of genteel, fashionable life."

Sometime during this period, Dolley, like her male contemporaries, began thinking of shaping her own historical legacy. She could not do so in the way they had. Not only had she no "papers" to publish, but as a woman, she could not openly embrace her political work or assert her own historical significance. But within all of the strictures placed on her sex, Dolley did make her own bids for posterity.

For instance, when in 1848 there was some talk about who actually saved the Washington painting, Dolley uncharacteristically addressed the issue in a letter to the newspaper. The family of Charles Carroll, who had been one of the men who tried to hurry Dolley out of the White House on that fateful day, had claimed in print that he was the portrait's rescuer. All of those years, she let published scandals and scurrilous accusations stand unchallenged, but this was too much. Even as she asserted herself in print, she downplayed her role and ascribed her motivations as the most selfless: "I acted thus because of my respect for General Washington—not that I felt a desire to gain laurels." Still, she added, "should there be a merit in remaining an hour in danger of life and liberty to save the likeness of anything, the merit in this case belongs to me."

She answered inquiries about the old White House, even helping interested parties ferret out possible paintings that might have been captured during the invasion. Dolley also collaborated with her old friend Margaret Bayard Smith to write an article about her as part of the four-volume *National Portrait Gallery of Distinguished Americans*, the only woman in Volume 3. For this, she supplied Margaret with a beautifully written copy (the only one that still exists) of the famous letter Dolley had written to her sister detailing her last days in the White House.

Again, unlike male politicians, Dolley would not dream of "intruding on the public notice"[3] with something so egotistical as a biography. It just wasn't done. But she talked to her niece, Mary Estelle Elizabeth Cutts, about her life and career, which Mary produced as a "memoir" in the years after her aunt's death. The use of the word "memoir" is problematic, as the events of the narrative took place long before Mary's birth, but these accounts are the closest we have to an autobiographical voice. The memoir stresses, amid slips about her active political work, that Dolley always valued and worked for unity for the nation and the capital city.

On July 12, 1849, at the age of eighty-one, Dolley Payne Todd Madison also died as she lived, in a crowd of friends and family—mostly women. Dolley had been connecting people with each other since she came to Washington City. In her early days as a political wife, she actively did so to aid her husband's goals of unity. During the time of the capital's crisis, she brought locals and officials together to save the city. In her later career, her mere presence reminded everyone who saw her that this experiment was one in which they were all in together.

Her death provided one last opportunity. Her body lay in state in her house on Lafayette Square and then in nearby St. John's Episcopal Church. Hundreds of mourners and admirers came to pay their respect to a woman they called both "Dolley" and "Queen." Hers was the largest state funeral ever seen in the city. All the branches of government closed, and as they had for over five decades, the government and the citizens of Washington laid aside partisan differences to be brought together by Dolley Madison.

At first glance, it would seem that the Madison goal of unity did not work. Dolley's drawing rooms may have contained partisan bitterness and doubtless aided individuals, but they did not stop the deterioration of that first try at a party system. Being the darling of diplomats—for instance, sending in cake and wine during a diplomatic contretemps— did not forestall the declaration of war between the United States and Great Britain.

But the way the explosion of nationalism in the aftermath of the war unified the country and solidified the capital city shows that the Madisons achieved a psychological victory. When the republic began, new Americans referred to their nation in the plural—the "United States of America are"; during the Madison era, reflecting their sense of unity, they made it singular—the "United States of America *is*." The unity that James imagined and Dolley strove for influenced how contemporaries and later generations thought about the war. In spite of impressive scholarship demonstrating the contrary, the conflict is still presented as the second war for independence and as a victory for the young nation.

Perhaps most important of all, in examining their efforts to build unity, one can reassess the gifts that both Madisons gave to the nation. Historians have long dismissed James Madison as a poor wartime leader because he did not lead aggressively. Perhaps modern scholars should appreciate James Madison's example of executive restraint. Though it did not prevail over more masculine political styles that became the hallmark of American politics, Dolley's model of bipartisan cooperation, civility, and empathy remains with us as a tool for a future politics. With modernity, it is clear that the only politics are psychological: how people feel about how they are ruled is the crucial factor. Dolley Madison took feelings seriously and, in the face of a political culture of anger and fear, cultivated that most crucial (and difficult to achieve) of capacities—the ability to see "the other" as fully human.

Recent years have seen a resurgence of interest in the founding fathers, so much so that the trend gained the nickname "Founders Chic." One explanation for the steady churning out of those massive biographies, and the eager buying of them by avid readers, is the desire for heroes and models. Aside from his work on the Constitution, President

James Madison seems an unlikely role model, let alone his wife, who held no official post and was "only" a hostess.

But as we move into our future, the need for unity—both in the nation and in the world—only assumes more urgency. In their own quest for unity, James and Dolley Madison provide modern Americans with examples of tolerance, civility, and empathy. A close look at the two and their personal and professional characters show us one way to be American. Dolley, in particular, demonstrates that the loftiest political goals are achieved not always through dramatic developments but in the way we live every day, in the smallest gestures of kindness and generosity. She reminds us that heroes are not always made in war; some are also made in peace.

Primary Sources
Making Your Own History

Now it's time for you to make a little history on your own. Historians are like detectives, finding and sifting through evidence in order to discern the truth. Like detectives, historians also weigh evidence, looking for holes in the story. Good historical detectives "listen" to everything told in pieces from the past, but they don't believe everything they hear.

All the letters here are from the Dolley Madison Digital Edition.

As we have seen in Chapter 10, in 1834 writer and reporter Margaret Bayard Smith contacted Dolley. She had been asked to write a piece about her for James B. Longacre and James Herring's four-volume *National Portrait Gallery of Distinguished Americans*. This was a prestigious volume and an honor for both women. Women rarely made an appearance in what their culture considered "History," either as authors or as subjects. Margaret was one of only a few women authors asked to pen a portrait, while Dolley was the only woman featured in Volume 3. Naturally, this interested Dolley, a woman who deliberately crafted a public persona for political uses.

This was her reply:

Dolley Payne Todd Madison to Margaret Bayard Smith,
31 August 1834

MONTPELLIER AUGT. 31ST. 1834.

—I have received with due sensibility my dear friend your kind letter of the 29th and can assure you that if a Biographical Sketch must be taken, its accomplishment by your pen, would be more agreeable to me than by any other to which such a task could be committed, being persuaded not only of its competency, but of the just dispositions by which it would be guided.

Dolley and Mary [Dolley's nieces] are now with us, but if I had known your wish as it regards my letters to them, and some of mine to their Mother I should have directed them to shew them to you without scruple—not . . . have thrown light on the early occurrences of my life but that they contain my unvarnished opinions and feelings on different subjects. As it is I will have them sent here, when the Girls return to the city, in order that I may select those at all worthy of your attention.

My family are all Virginians except myself, who was born in N. Carolina whilst my Parents were there on a visit of one year, to an Uncle. Their families on both sides, were among the most respectable and they, becoming members of the society of friends soon after their Marriage manumitted their Slaves, and left this state for that of Pennsylvania, bearing with them their children to be educated in their religion—I beleive my age at that time was 11. or 12 years—I was educated in Philadelphia where I was married to Mr Todd in 1790, and to Mr. Madison in 94, when I returned with him to the soil of my Father, and to Washington, where you have already traced me with the kindness of a Sister. In the year 91, and after the death of my Father, my Mother received into her house some Gentlemen as boarders—and in 93 she left Philadelphia to reside with her daughter Washington—afterwards, with my Sister Jackson and occasionally with me. I am sensible that this, is but a general answer to yours. Should any particular information be desired, I will endeaver to furnish it.

Your constant friend

D. P. M.

* * *

Dolley had known Margaret for over thirty years. Though this letter seems quite friendly, the following excerpt from a letter Dolley wrote to her younger sister, in which she describes Margaret, suggests something else.

Dolley Payne Todd Madison to Anna Payne Cutts, 6 June 1829

6TH. JUNE 29.

. . . She is a *curious* body—& tho she appears affectinate & frank, I think she is *dangerious*.

* * *

From her initial reply, Dolley also seems to indicate her cooperation, offering to enlist her nieces' help in collecting materials that they could take back to Margaret in Washington. Indeed, a few months after Margaret's initial communication, Dolley seems to take an active hand in culling through material. She is also already expressing worries.

Dolley Payne Todd Madison to Mary Estelle Elizabeth Cutts, October [1834]

OCTOR [1834]

I had indeed waited with impatience for an acknowledgement of my letter & 45$ by Mrs R. or rather by Mrs Cooledge who knew the money was Enclosed as she read it, on the outside—but 'tis past & safe in your hands. Now dearest I must call your attention to a few points— after congratulating Madisons Ellen on the birth of their fine daughter, with my best wishes for their all doing well, so tell them, both from me. In the first place—I *fear* that you have not given Mrs Smith the extract of a letter I wrote my sister, finished the day of the destruction of the P. s House—If you have lost it, or omitted to give it to her, it *will be* much to my injury, as the original is nearly torn to *bits* by the mice with several others, describing what followed—2d. did you rece. the residue of my letters to you & Dolley & lend them to Mrs Smith for her perusal? I *pray* you to do these things.

Dolley Payne Todd Madison to Mary Estelle Elizabeth Cutts, 10 March 1835

MONTPELIER 10TH. MARCH 1835

I rejoiced at the pleasant visit you made to Kalarama, dearst Mary, as well as at hearing of the health and enjoyments of my dear Dolley and yourself during the *hard* winter. I was anxious to write and tell you of Miss Martineau's visit, and how much we were pleased with her enlightened conversation and unassuming manners—her lively little friend Miss Jeffrys also, but weak eyes! even now, I can scarcely write five minutes together, so that I must hasten to day as much as I can now, and do more when they are better. Dear good Mrs. Smith will have so few incidents to make her Biography interesting that I ought to *tremble* for it (between you and I).

Dolley Payne Todd Madison to Mary Estelle Elizabeth Cutts, 2 December 1834

2D. DECR. 34.

Be assured sweet Mary that when I am silent to D, & you, it is because I cannot write—At this moment my eyes are half closed—cold, added to their habitual weakness, has made me thus long in replying to your acceptable letters—I recd. them safe, & must ever think highly of your heart (as I always have done) when I recollect how much you have done for that dr brother, who has hitherto been unfortunate, but who I trust will now flourish in defiance of all sorts of enimies—I recd. your bonit pattern & have cut & made one by it of black Velvet—Give my kind love to Mrs Smith & tell her It wd. give me pleasure to do what she recommends, & that I hope it will not be long before I make the effort, tho' I can not promise much, as I cannot give her anything of importance *in my own Eyes*. I have other letters beside the one the extract was taken from—which continues the *little* history of War times, & *my especial difficulties*; but egotism is so repugnant to my nature that I *shrink* from recording my own feelings, acts or doings—You can *repeat this* to Mrs S. whom I consider a kind friend, & amiable lady.

The letter continues, but at the end Dolley returns to the topic of "Mrs. Smith."

I keep Mrs. Smiths note to you a little longer I wish you'd both visit her, as she invites &c &c.

* * *

Dolley also makes excuses to Margaret.

Dolley Payne Todd Madison to Margaret Bayard Smith, 17 January 1835

MONTPELLIER JANY. 17. 1835.

—Be assured my dear friend that we reciprocate all the good wishes which your letter has so kindly conveyed to us this day—for yourself— Mr Smith and your amiable family—and truly, your observations on new acquaintances accord also, with my feelings on the subject—my experience teaches, that our hearts recur and cling to early attachments, as the most happy of our lives. I ought now to offer many apologies for my silence, and if I was not acquainted with your goodness and for- bearance—I should despair of forgiveness—but I trust in a simple state- ment of facts to shew you that my delinquency has not proceeded from want of love, and confidence in your friendship, nor am I without ex- planations, which will at least mitigate it. My letters to my Sister Todd at the closing scenes of the War, happen to be with her in Kentucky, and I was unwilling to have them exposed to the Mail, if I had been sure of their arrival in time, and that they contained any thing worthy of being extracted. I might plead also my constant engagements of dif- ferent sorts at home, which have not permitted me to search over pa- pers, and bring my mind to the revisal of scenes, or circumstances that might possibly throw a faint interest over a recital of them, and lastly I must in candour say, that I have felt more than a mere reluctance in being a Judge and witness, of incidents if existing, that might be wor- thy of the use to be made of them.

* * *

In the end, Dolley shares almost nothing with Margaret, except a "good picture" of herself and one letter. This is the letter she refers to several times as either being in Kentucky, and thus out of her hands, or being nibbled by mice in Washington. This letter is her most famous—written to her sister Lucy on August 24, 1814, the last day of the first White House. No original of this exists; we have only Margaret's transcription and an obviously fair copy in Dolley's best penmanship.

Here is the letter:

Dolley Payne Todd Madison to Lucy Payne Washington Todd, 23 August 1814

TUESDAY AUGT. 23D. 1814.

Dear Sister.

—My husband left me yesterday morng. to join Gen. Winder. He enquired anxiously whether I had courage, or firmness to remain in the President's house until his return, on the morrow, or succeeding day, and on my assurance that I had no fear but for him and the success of our army, he left me, beseeching me to take care of myself, and of the cabinet papers, public and private. I have since recd. two despatches from him, written with a pencil; the last is alarming, because he desires I should be ready at a moment's warning to enter my carriage and leave the city; that the enemy seemed stronger than had been reported and that it might happen that they would reach the city, with intention to destroy it. X X X

X X X I am accordingly ready; I have pressed as many cabinet papers into trunks as to fill one carriage; our private property must be sacrificed, as it is impossible to procure wagons for its transportation. I am determined not to go myself until I see Mr. Madison safe, and he can accompany me, as I hear of much hostility towards him, X X X disaffection stalks around us.

X X X X X My friends and acquaintances are all gone; Even Col. C— with his hundred men, who were stationed as a guard in the enclosure.

X X French John (a faithful domestic,) with his usual activity and resolution, offers to spike the cannon at the gate, and to lay a train of powder which would blow up the British, should they enter the house. To the last proposition I positively object, without being able, however, to make him understand why all advantages in war may not be taken.

Wednesday morng., twelve O'clock. Since sunrise I have been turning my spy glass in every direction and watching with unwearied anxiety, hoping to discern the approach of my dear husband and his friends; but, alas, I can descry only groups of military wandering in all directions, as if there was a lack of arms, or of spirit to fight for their own firesides!

Three O'clock. Will you believe it, my Sister? We have had a battle or skirmish near Bladensburg, and I am still here within sound of the cannon! Mr. Madison comes not; may God protect him! Two messengers covered with dust, come to bid me fly; but I wait for him. X X X At this late hour a wagon has been procured, I have had it filled with the plate and most valuable portable articles belonging to the house; whether it will reach its destination; the Bank of Maryland, or fall into the hands of British soldiery, events must determine.

Our kind friend, Mr. Carroll, has come to hasten my departure, and is in a very bad humor with me because I insist on waiting until the large picture of Gen. Washington is secured, and it requires to be unscrewed from the wall. This process was found too tedious for these perilous moments; I have ordered the frame to be broken, and the canvass taken out it is done, and the precious portrait placed in the hands of two gentlemen of New York, for safe keeping. And now, dear sister, I must leave this house, or the retreating army will make me a prisoner in it, by filling up the road I am directed to take. When I shall again write you, or where I shall be tomorrow, I cannot tell!!

Faced with Dolley's lack of cooperation, Margaret's article consists of this letter and her own recollections. Read the final product—and see the "good picture" of Dolley—on Google Books using the search term "Dolley Madison National Portrait Gallery of Distinguished Americans."

* * *

Let's allow Margaret Bayard Smith to have the final word. In a letter dated February 6, 1836, Margaret writes to her sister Maria Bayard Boyd: "In the last Portrait gallery—you will see my memoir of Mrs. Madison— all I say is true—but I have not of course told the whole truth."

STUDY QUESTIONS

1. In the primary source document, what do you make of the correspondence around Margaret Bayard Smith's attempts to write an entry about Dolley Madison? Can you spot the lies in Dolley's initial reply? Is she afraid of not being interesting enough or too interesting? Do you have any doubts about the authenticity of the famous 1814 letter?

2. In Chapter 2, the author makes the case that Dolley and James were "a perfect match." In what ways did their political goals and styles contrast and complement each other?

3. What is the "unofficial sphere," and how does it work in politics?

4. The political culture of the early republic was a particularly masculine one. How did Dolley's work from the unofficial sphere mitigate the antipathy and violence?

5. The author discusses the role of "psychological politics" (see especially Chapter 10). What does that mean in this context? Do you find her point persuasive?

6. In the end, in what ways were Dolley and James successful in their quest for unity? Where did they fail?

7. According to the author, Dolley and James left models for governance. What are they, and can you imagine how they could be used today?

NOTES AND
BIBLIOGRAPHY

All material to and from Dolley Payne Todd Madison (DPTM) is cited as such and can be found in the Dolley Madison Digital Edition (Rotunda—the Electronic Imprint of the University of Virginia Press, rotunda.upress.virginia.edu/dmde/). Any emphasis in the quoted material is in the original source. All other quotations are cited from the secondary works in which they appear. See the Secondary Sources section for full bibliographic information for each abbreviated source cited in the notes.

CHAPTER 1

1. Ketcham, *JM*, 612; Allgor, *APU*, 342, 339–340; DPTM to Hannah Nicholson Gallatin [March 5, 1815]; DPTM to Edward Coles, March 6, 1816; Allgor, *APU*, 334.
2. Allgor, *APU*, 336–337; Rossiter, *Federalist Papers*, 78; McCoy, *Last*, 48, 164.
3. McCoy, *Last*, 11–12, 17, 19, 22–23.
4. Allgor, *APU*, 340–341; Lucia Alice von Kantzow to DPTM, June 28, 1818.

CHAPTER 2

1. Allgor, *APU*, 250; Allgor, *PP*, 90; Allgor, *Queen*, 93–94; DPTM to Eliza Collins Lee, Sept. 16, 1794.
2. Allgor, *Queen*, 90.
3. DPTM to Anna Payne Cutts, Aug. 19, 1805.
4. Allgor, *Queen*, 90.

CHAPTER 3

1. Ketcham, *JM*, 409; Allgor, *APU*, 38, 41–43.
2. Allgor, *APU*, 47–48, 57, 42, 146.
3. Allgor, *APU*, 69, 64, 44.

4. Allgor, *APU*, 74–76, 72–73.
5. Allgor, *APU*, 76.

CHAPTER 4

1. Allgor, *APU*, 60; DPTM to Anna Payne Cutts, May 22, June 4, 1805; DPTM to Anna Payne Cutts, April 26, 1804.
2. Allgor, *Queen*, 138–139; Allgor, *APU*, 83.
3. Allgor, *APU*, 84, 85; Lester, *Redivivus*, 31–32.
4. Allgor, *APU*, 86, 87, 89.
5. Allgor, *APU*, 90, 92, 69, 93–94.
6. Allgor, *APU*, 94.
7. DPTM to Anna Payne Cutts, May 25, June 4, 1804; Edward Thornton to DPTM, circa 1803–1804.

CHAPTER 5

1. DPTM to Anna Payne Cutts [May 8, 1804], June 4 [1805]; DPTM to James Madison, Oct. 26, 1805, Nov. 1 [1805]; James Madison to DPTM, Nov. [19–20], 1805, [Nov. 6, 1805]; DPTM to James Madison, Nov. 12, 1805; DPTM to Eliza Collins Lee, Feb. 26, 1808.
2. Allgor, *APU*, 129, 132–135, 144.
3. DPTM to Anna Payne Cutts, June 3 [1808]; Allgor, *APU*, 122; Allgor, *Queen*, 108.
4. Allgor, *APU*, 178–179; Allgor, *PP*, 69.
5. Allgor, *APU*, 157; Mary Hazelhurst Latrobe to DPTM, April 12 [1809]; Benjamin Henry Latrobe to DPTM, March 29, March 22, April 21, 1809; Allgor, *APU*, 162.
6. Benjamin Henry Latrobe to DPTM, Sept. 8, 1809; DPTM to Benjamin Henry Latrobe, Sept. 12, 1809; Allgor, *APU*, 168.

CHAPTER 6

1. Allgor, *APU*, 173–174; Allgor, *PP*, 76; Allgor, *APU*, 189.
2. Allgor, *APU*, 190; DPTM to Ruth Baldwin Barlow, Nov. 15, 1811; DPTM to James Taylor, March 13 [1811]; Allgor, *APU*, 194; DPTM to Anna Payne Cutts [circa March 27, 1812]; Allgor, *PP*, 77.
3. Allgor, *APU*, 197, 191, 193–194, 249; Allgor *PP*, 78.
4. DPTM to Anna Payne Cutts [circa March 1812]; Allgor, *APU*, 267.
5. Allgor, *APU*, 199, 174.

CHAPTER 7

1. Allgor, *APU*, 244, 242.
2. Allgor, *APU*, 236, 237, 239.
3. Allgor, *APU*, 243, 190, 240, 244, 243.

4. Allgor, *APU*, 195, 246, 247, 234; Allgor, *Queen*, 108, 110, 115; Allgor, *APU*, 174.
5. Allgor, *APU*, 250, 247–248, 233, 245.

CHAPTER 8

1. Allgor, *APU*, 232, 274; Allgor, *Queen*, 121.
2. DPTM to Phoebe Pemberton Morris [circa Oct. 17, 1812]; Allgor, *APU*, 290, 291; DPTM to Edward Coles, June 10, 1813, Aug. 31 [1812]; Allgor, *APU*, 293–294.
3. Allgor, *APU*, 292, 293; Allgor, *Queen*, 119–120; DPTM to Phoebe Pemberton Morris, Aug. 16, 1812; Allgor, *APU*, 306; DPTM to Edward Coles, May 13, 1813; Allgor, *APU*, 307.
4. Allgor, *APU*, 309; DPTM to John Payne Todd, Aug. 6, 1814; DPTM to Hannah Nicholson Gallatin, July 28, Aug. 6, 1814; DPTM to Edward Coles, May 13, 1813.

CHAPTER 9

1. DPTM to Lucy Payne Washington, Aug. 23, 1814; Anna Payne Cutts to DPTM [circa Aug. 23, 1814]; Eleanor Jones to DPTM, Aug. 24, 1814; Allgor, *APU*, 313; 314.
2. Allgor, *APU*, 315, 316, 318, 319, 320, 321.
3. Allgor, *APU*, 322, 324, 325.
4. DPTM to Hannah Nicholson Gallatin, Jan. 14, 1815; Allgor, *APU*, 329; DPTM to Edward Coles, March 5, 1816; Margaret Bayard Smith to Jane Bayard Fitzpatrick, Feb. 7, 1817; Allgor, *APU*, 328, 333, 334.

CHAPTER 10

1. McCoy, *Last*, 108; Allgor, *APU*, 365–366, 367.
2. Allgor, *APU*, 387, 360, 364.
3. DPTM to Richard Cutts, July 5, 1836; DPTM to Andrew Jackson [Aug. 20, 1836]; Allgor, *APU*, 379, 395; DPTM to Robert G. L. De Peyster, Feb. 11, 1848.

SECONDARY SOURCES

Discussions of Dolley Madison can be found in many First Lady compilations, but for the most part, these entries do not follow modern scholarly standards, merely repeating legends and oft-circulated tales. This book draws on Catherine Allgor, *A Perfect Union: Dolley Madison and the Creation of the American Nation* (New York: Henry Holt, 2006) (in notes *APU*), and the essays in David B. Mattern and Holly C. Shulman, *The Selected Letters of Dolley Payne Madison* (Charlottesville: University of Virginia Press, 2003). A transcription of Mary Cutts's memoir of her aunt appears in Catherine Allgor, ed., *The Queen of America: Mary Cutts's Life of Dolley Madison*, Jeffersonian America (Charlottesville: University of Virginia Press, 2012) (in notes *Queen*).

Chapters 1 and 2 introduce James Madison. The best full-scale biography of him is Ralph Ketcham, *James Madison* (Charlottesville: University Press of Virginia, 1990) (in notes *JM*). More focused treatments of James Madison's political thought and practices can be found in Garry Wills, *James Madison* (New York: Henry Holt, 2002), and Jack N. Rakove, *James Madison and the Creation of the American Republic* (New York: Longman, 2006). Drew R. McCoy, *The Last of the Fathers: James Madison and the Republican Legacy* (Cambridge: Cambridge University Press, 1989) (in notes *Last*), is an excellent examination of the retirement years. There are many fine editions of *The Federalist Papers*; the one used for this book is Clinton Rossiter, *The Federalist Papers* (New York: Signet, 2003). James Madison's enslaved valet, Paul Jennings, is one of the most important sources we have for James's private life and character. Jennings's own life is traced in Elizabeth Dowling Taylor, *A Slave in the White House: Paul Jennings and the Madisons* (New York: Palgrave Macmillan, 2012).

Chapter 2 also discusses the "woman question." For more, see Linda Kerber, *Women of the Republic: Intellect and Ideology in Revolutionary America* (Chapel Hill: University of North Carolina Press, 1980), and Jan Lewis, "The Republican Wife," *William and Mary Quarterly* 44 (October 1987): 689–721. Rosemarie Zagarri, "Morals, Manners, and the Republican Mother," *American Quarterly* 44 (June 1992): 192–215, discusses the influence of the Scottish Enlightenment. See also Rosemarie Zagarri, *Revolutionary Backlash: Women and Politics in the Early American Republic* (Philadelphia: University of Pennsylvania Press, 2008).

The literature around the founding of early Washington is large and various, but a few good studies are Kenneth R. Bowling, *Creating the Federal City, 1774–1800: Potomac Fever* (Washington, DC: American Institute of Architects Press, 1988); Barbara Carson, *Ambitious Appetites: Dining, Behavior, and Patterns of Consumption in Federal Washington* (Washington, DC: American Institute of Architects Press, 1990); and Bob Arnebeck, *Through A Fiery Trial: Building Washington, 1790–1800* (Lanham, MD: Madison Books, 1991). The classic work is James Sterling Young, *The Washington Community, 1800–1828* (New York: Columbia University Press, 1966).

There is also a good depiction of capital society and Jefferson in Catherine Allgor, *Parlor Politics: In Which the Ladies of Washington Help Build a City and a Government* (Charlottesville: University Press of Virginia, 2000) (in notes *PP*). For the larger political culture, including an arresting discussion of Jefferson, see Joseph J. Ellis, *Founding Brothers: The Revolutionary Generation* (New York: Knopf, 2000). For the overheated political violence of the early republic, see Joanne B. Freeman, *Affairs of Honor: National Politics in the New Republic* (New Haven, CT: Yale University Press, 2001). On fears of disunion, see Elizabeth R. Varon, *Disunion! The Coming of the American Civil War, 1789–1859* (Chapel Hill: University of North Carolina Press, 2010).

Malcolm Lester, *Anthony Merry Redivivus: A Reappraisal of the British Minister to the United States, 1803–6* (Charlottesville: University of Virginia Press, 1978) (in notes *Redivivus*), discusses the Merry Affair of Chapter 4, as does Allgor, *Parlor Politics*. The War of 1812 is analyzed in many treatments of the era. Donald R. Hickey, *The War of 1812: A Short History* (Champaign: University of Illinois Press, 1995), is an abridgment of his larger work. Anthony S. Pitch, *The Burning of Washington: The British Invasion of 1814* (Annapolis: Naval Institute Press, 1998), supplies an in-depth discussion of the invasion. In time for the commemoration of the bicentennial of the War of 1812, the editor of the Papers of

James Madison, J. C. A. Stagg, has written *The War of 1812: Conflict for a Continent* (Cambridge: Cambridge University Press, 2012).

For the fist play produced in America, see: Cynthia A. Kierner and Royall Tyler, *The Contrast: Manners, Morals, and Authority in the Early American Republic* (New York: New York University Press, 2007).

PRIMARY SOURCES

The Dolley Madison Digital Edition (rotunda.upress.virginia.edu/dmde/) is a database for all of Dolley's papers, including letters to and from Dolley Madison, and is available in many libraries. The collection is still growing and will expand to include all primary sources concerning Dolley. The editors of the DMDE also administer the Dolley Madison Project at www2.vcdh.virginia.edu/madison/.

Printed primary sources include Rosalie Stier Calvert, *Mistress of Riversdale: The Plantation Letters of Rosalie Stier Calvert*, edited and translated by Margaret Law Callcott (Baltimore: Johns Hopkins University Press, 1991); Catharine Mitchill, "Catharine Mitchill's Letters from Washington, 1806–1812," edited by Carolyn Hoover Sung, *Quarterly Journal of the Library of Congress* 34, no. 3 (July 1977): 171–189; and Margaret Bayard Smith, *The First Forty Years of Washington Society Portrayed by the Family Letters of Mrs. Samuel Harrison Smith*, Cornell University Library Digital Collections (1906; reprint, Charleston, SC: Nabu Press, 2010) (in notes *First Forty*).

INDEX

and Dolley's drawing rooms, 88
and election of 1808, 65–66, 70
on foreign relations, 52
Madison's goal for, 135
and Merry Affair, 60
on virtue as public good, 38
women's role, 34
Republicanism
aversion to monarchy, 10–11, 38–39,
89–90, 94, 98–99, 104
moving beyond to democracy, 135
as ruling theory of American
Revolution, 10–11
and societal reform, 30
transmutation through court culture,
91
women's role, 67
Residence Act (1790), 32
Revolutionary War. *See* American
Revolution
Ritual, founders eschewal of, 89–90
Rives, Judith Walker, 141–142
Rives, William Cabell, 141–142
Roberts, Jonathan, 88, 102

Scottish Enlightenment, 31
Seaton, Sarah Gales, 81, 99, 110, 115
Sexual innuendoes against James and
Dolley, 60, 67–68
Sioussat, "French John," 122, 124
Slaves and slavery
abolition movement, 147
American views on, 135–136
claiming rights, 136
Congress on new states admission to
United States, 137–139
and Constitution of the United States,
21, 136–137
Dolley's views, 23, 36, 139–140
James's views, 12–13, 20–21, 137–139
Quaker view, 25
Smith, James, 123
Smith, Margaret Bayard
about, 41–42

article on Dolley, 148, 151–153,
155–156, 157
on calling duties, 113
on Dolley, 105, 110, 126, 132
on Dolley's sociability, 66–67
on Elizabeth Merry, 59
on moving Washington City, 128
on senator's and judge's first sight of a
piano, 70–71
on War of 1812, 117, 133
and Washington Female Orphan
Asylum, 129
Smith, Samuel Harrison, 41, 44
Smith, Susan, 71
Snuff and snuffbox, 44, 110
Social order
and Americans' lack of graces,
70–71
attendance at social events, 103
coverture of women, 23–24, 112
and drawing room regularity, 83–84
premium on masculinity, 18–19
republican mothers, 30–31
slavery as maintenance of, 138
Socializing as unofficial sphere of
politics, 77, 81–86, 112, 130. *See
also* drawing room events
Spain
diplomat to US, 50–51, 56, 57, 60
and Louisiana Purchase, 50–51
Spheres of political activity, 77. *See also*
unofficial sphere of politics
"Star-Spangled Banner, The" (Key),
125–126
States rights
individual rights and, 20, 33–34
Kentucky and Virginia Resolutions,
35
Republican vs. Federalist on, 33–34
Stevens, John, 78
Stevens, Robert, 78–79
Stockton, Annis Boudinot, 31
Stuart, Charlotte Coates, 65
Stuart, Gilbert, 123